Editor-in-Chief and Founder:
  Lyndon H. LaRouche, Jr.
Editorial Board: *Lyndon H. LaRouche, Jr. , Helga
  Zepp-LaRouche, Robert Ingraham, Tony
  Papert, Gerald Rose, Dennis Small, Jeffrey
  Steinberg, William Wertz*
Co-Editors: *Robert Ingraham, Tony Papert*
Technology: *Marsha Freeman*
Transcriptions: *Katherine Notley*
Ebooks: *Richard Burden*
Graphics: *Alan Yue*
Photos: *Stuart Lewis*
Circulation Manager: *Stanley Ezrol*

INTELLIGENCE DIRECTORS
Economics: *Marcia Merry Baker, Paul Gallagher*
History: *Anton Chaitkin*
Ibero-America: *Dennis Small*
Russia and Eastern Europe: *Rachel Douglas*
United States: *Debra Freeman*

INTERNATIONAL BUREAUS
Bogotá: *Miriam Redondo*
Berlin: *Rainer Apel*
Copenhagen: *Tom Gillesberg*
Lima: *Sara Madueño*
Melbourne: *Robert Barwick*
Mexico City: *Gerardo Castilleja Chávez*
New Delhi: *Ramtanu Maitra*
Paris: *Christine Bierre*
Stockholm: *Ulf Sandmark*
United Nations, N.Y.C.: *Leni Rubinstein*
Washington, D.C.: *William Jones*
Wiesbaden: *Göran Haglund*

ON THE WEB
e-mail: eirns@larouchepub.com
www.larouchepub.com
www.executiveintelligencereview.com
www.larouchepub.com/eiw
Webmaster: *John Sigerson*
Assistant Webmaster: *George Hollis*
Editor, Arabic-language edition: *Hussein Askary*

EIR (ISSN 0273-6314) *is published weekly
(50 issues), by EIR News Service, Inc.,
P.O. Box 17390, Washington, D.C. 20041-0390.
(703) 297-8434*

European Headquarters: E.I.R. GmbH, Postfach
Bahnstrasse 9a, D-65205, Wiesbaden, Germany
Tel: 49-611-73650
Homepage: http://www.eir.de
e-mail: info@eir.de
Director: Georg Neudecker

Montreal, Canada: 514-461-1557
eir@eircanada.ca

Denmark: EIR - Denmark, Sankt Knuds Vej 11,
basement left, DK-1903 Frederiksberg, Denmark.
Tel.: +45 35 43 60 40, Fax: +45 35 43 87 57. e-mail:
eirdk@hotmail.com.

Mexico City: EIR, Sor Juana Inés de la Cruz 242-2
Col. Agricultura C.P. 11360
Delegación M. Hidalgo, México D.F.
Tel. (5525) 5318-2301
eirmexico@gmail.com

Copyright: ©2018 EIR News Service. All rights
reserved. Reproduction in whole or in part without
permission strictly prohibited.

Canada Post Publication Sales Agreement
#40683579

Postmaster: Send all address changes to *EIR*, P.O.
Box 17390, Washington, D.C. 20041-0390.

Signed articles in *EIR* represent the views of the authors,
and not necessarily those of the Editorial Board.

A Great Change Comes for Africa

EIR Contents

www.larouchepub.com Volume 45, Number 37, September 14, 2018

Xinhua/Ju Peng

Will U.S. Forces Assist Al Qaeda Terrorist Butchers in Syria?

Interview with Virginia State Senator Richard Black on His Fact-Finding Mission to Syria

https://www.youtube.com/watch?v=YZeZ_OZAaRM

LAROUCHE PAC STATEMENT

Major British Effort Now Underway To Impeach Trump 'Sooner Rather than Later'

It's Open Sedition: Now Is the Time To Organize the Counter-Coup

by Barbara Boyd

Sept. 6—If you have been following the ongoing coup against the President, you know by now that its "events" are not things in themselves; they are part of a constructed narrative, a British information warfare effort whose objective is to drive this President from office. So it is with the most recent series of "events": the conviction of Paul Manafort and the guilty plea of Michael Cohen, John Mc-Cain's absurd and orchestrated funeral, Bob Woodward's outrageous new round of political pornography aimed at the President, and now, the anonymous op-ed from a "senior official" in the Trump Administration, published on the Sept. 5 Opinion page of the *New York Times*.

The gutless author of the *New York Times* op-ed claims to be a member of the "resistance" inside the Administration and doubles down on Woodward's ludicrous fake portrait of the President as an unhinged child from whom the nation must be protected. The *Times* says it is protecting the identity of this creep to save his or her job, to wit, to ensure that he or she can continue outright sedition against the President of the United States. The op-ed lauds John McCain and explicitly references the President's alleged rage at being boxed into

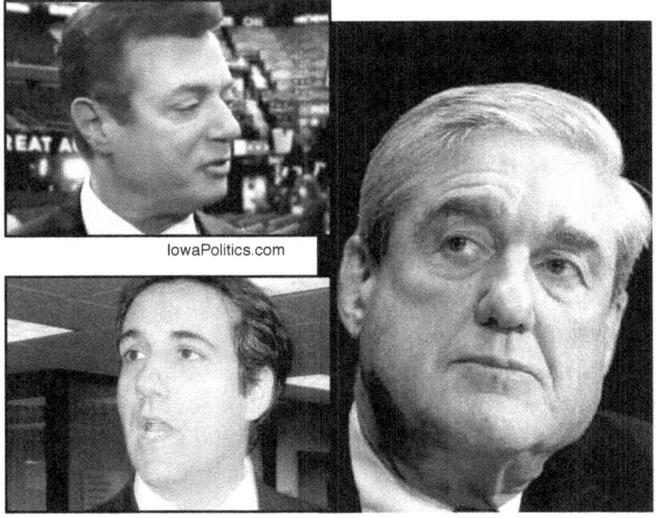

While Special Counsel Robert Mueller (center left) picked the "low-hanging fruit" in the conviction of Paul Manafort (upper left) and the guilty plea of Michael Cohen (lower left), Theresa May (right) says her government has now identified and charged the Russians (far right) who poisoned the Skirpals.

adding more sanctions against Russia based on the Sergei Skripal poisoning hoax in Great Britain.

As Glenn Greenwald appropriately commented, "The irony in the op-ed from the *New York Times*'s anonymous White House coward is glaring and massive: s/he accuses Trump of being 'anti-democratic' while boasting of membership in an unelected cabal that covertly imposes their own ideology with zero democratic accountability, mandate or transparency."

At the same time, the British have undertaken new strategic provocations against Russia, both carrying the label "poison." Charges were announced Sept. 5 by Theresa May against two "Russians" for the Skripal poisoning. A new false flag chemical attack in Syria, which is to be blamed on Bashar al-Assad and Vladimir Putin, has also been in the works for several days. Undoubtedly the Brits will now escalate, calling for new military actions against Russia and threatening the world with a new war. Senator Chuck Schumer gave the game away over the weekend when he said that impeachment must come now, "sooner rather than later."

To accomplish this, a whole series of events has been planned between now and the U.S. midterm elections. At the very least, they aim to depress and suppress the turnout of pro-Trump voters and jack up the increasingly Jacobin base of the Democratic Party. God only knows what will launch from this crowd if the now imminent financial collapse occurs, in Schumer's words, "sooner rather than later."

A Prelude to Nuclear War

Former German Assistant Defense Minister Willy Wimmer, in a strongly worded statement published September 3, outlined the stakes precisely. If the Democrats take the House in the November midterm elections and impeach the President, Wimmer warns, it would be the prelude to a nuclear war against Russia, the foremost enemy of the circles identified with the names of John McCain and Hillary Clinton. The buildup for the confrontation has been assiduously pursued in Europe during recent years, he wrote, so that the removal of Trump from office "would be the breaking of the dam which is keeping the peace alive."

This is not to say that the President's enemies are winning. In fact, they are totally exposed and increasingly desperate, having tried just about everything to oust this President for the last two years, to no avail. Each new attack exposes more and more of the appara-

tus and machinery by which the U.S. population was tamed following 9/11 and the financial crash of 2008, prior to their revolt in the 2016 presidential election. The backfire potential in these crazed actions is enormous and will only stoke the fire that is still very much alive in the American population.

So, organize, vote, convince your friends and neighbors to vote, and register new voters. These aspiring viceroys stand on the verge of a huge defeat if we do our job. Do it with humor and ridicule directed toward the "resistance," the overrated, self-important professional windbags who already have done almost irreparable damage to our republic under Bush and Obama and now have the audacity to ask for a return to their insane policies.

The current round of potentially deadly nonsense began right after the President was experiencing a notable uptick in his approval level, even within the rigged polls, and as the "blue wave" forecast for the midterm elections was fading. Anyone not living in a cave knows that if the Democrats prevail in the midterms, the President's impeachment will be launched in the House with the very corrupt Special Counsel Robert Mueller providing the pretext. As we have repeatedly stated, the reason for this coup is very clear: Trump threatens the worldwide Anglo-Dutch monetarist empire, the sponsors of what people mistakenly call the Deep State, or the Establishment.

At this very moment, that Empire teeters on the edge of a new and thunderous financial collapse. At the same time, a new paradigm of relations among nations, under the rubric of China's Belt and Road Initiative, is proceeding, rapidly, to replace the decadent Anglo-Dutch Empire and its grip on the world's finances and resources. Instead of being kept in poverty through free trade, outsourcing, cheap labor, and austerity, formerly impoverished nations and continents are now being developed with modern infrastructure. In the past few days, at the summit of the Forum on China-Africa Cooperation, huge new infrastructure and development initiatives were announced between China and most countries on the African continent.

Trump is a threat because his endorsement of the American System of political economy, fundamental scientific research and space exploration, and his pledge to build large-scale infrastructure, signals the very real possibility of an entirely new order of international relationships in which China, Russia, the United States, and others collaborate on physical development of the world. Trump has absolutely no loyalty to the failed old order of permanent war, Wall Street bailouts, and post-industrial society. This is why, according to Schumer, the Senator from Wall Street, impeachment must occur "sooner rather than later."

Now, let's take these recent propaganda stunts in reverse order, to better unwind their intended cascade effect on the popular mind.

Woodward, the *Post,* and the *New York Times*

Forget about Bob Woodward, the pompous darling of the Washington establishment, whom the press have loved to celebrate ever since he and Carl Bernstein functioned as human dead drops for the leaks from the FBI and others that brought down Richard Nixon. In all of his books, Woodward has always relied on anonymous sources, primarily from the U.S. intelligence community that leaks salacious bits of gossip to him for their own political and institutional purposes. Christopher Hitchens famously called Woodward "the stenographer for the rich and the powerful."

In the case of George W. Bush, that meant propping up and giving substance to perhaps the most mentally vacant President in U.S. history and supporting the Iraq War and the other disastrous military interventions, which wrecked the U.S. military and much of Southwest Asia. Woodward's much ballyhooed account of a deathbed conversation with former CIA Director Bill Casey has been widely debunked as fabricated and drew a rare public rebuke from President Ronald Reagan who called Woodward an outright liar. This is why President Trump is right to ask whether the *New York Times*'s "senior Trump official" actually exists or is simply another Woodward "source." Woodward's book on the 2008 bailout of Wall Street, following the collapse which broke most of the country and destroyed our middle class, is a vicious lie, painting the totally corrupted officials of the Bush and Obama administrations as well-intentioned public servants.

The late, great actual investigative reporter, Robert Parry, took Woodward to task for not reporting Richard Nixon's crime that caused the Watergate cover up: Nixon's deliberate sabotage, using Henry Kissinger and

Bob Woodward's reporting has been questioned before. | REUTERS

6 Bob Woodward controversies

2. CIA Director William Casey's deathbed scene

Woodward claimed in his book "Veil: The Secret Wars of the CIA 1981-1987" that Casey admitted on his deathbed that he had known about the diversion of Iran arms sale money to the Contras.

others, to subvert the Vietnam Paris peace talks, prolonging the Vietnam War for years in order to win the 1968 presidential election. This successful game cost thousands of U.S. and Vietnamese lives. Woodward had the story at the time, exclusively, but chose not to report it.

Writer Joan Didion best summed up Woodward and his "work" in a famous essay published in the Sept.1996 *New York Review of Books.* She said that after Watergate, "measurable cerebral activity" in Woodward's books was virtually absent, and that the books have "a scrupulous passivity, an agreement to cover the story *not as it is occurring but as it is presented, which is to say as it is manufactured.*" She calls his method "political pornography."

The *Washington Post*—now in the hands of Resist member and pirate capitalist Jeff Bezos—was, for years, owned by the Graham family and functioned purposely throughout the post-World War II period as a psychological warfare and propaganda vehicle for the CIA and intelligence community. Complementing the *Times*'s effort at sedition, the *Post* coverage of the op-ed by the gutless "senior official" had the headline, "Sleeper Cells Have Now Awoken."

As for the *New York Times*—well, anyone who is literate can cite its early support for Mussolini and Hitler and its history as the propaganda vehicle of

Radio Free Europe/Radio Liberty

Former Presidents Barack Obama (front left), George W. Bush (front center), and Bill Clinton (front right), united in their eulogy of their deceased comrade Sen. John McCain, and in their war against President Trump, attending McCain's televised funeral extravaganza at the National Cathedral, Washington, D.C., Sept. 1, 2018.

record for Wall Street and the City of London. The *Post* and the *Times* have been outpaced only by CNN and MSNBC as purveyors of hate against this President.

The McCain Death Extravaganza

John McCain deserved a decent funeral based on his war record and his long, if destructive, public service. McCain and others in Washington's arrogant and narcissistic elite decided before his death, however, to use his demise to advance the coup against the President, and to make claims about the late Senator and themselves which are totally and utterly false and delusional. The funeral was a national media extravaganza, achieving a status normally enjoyed only by former Presidents.

It was, according to *New Yorker* magazine, also the "biggest resistance meeting yet." President Donald Trump was not invited, so that the cowards in the funeral crowd, Barack Obama, and George W. Bush, could freely take potshots at the President. McCain picked these leaders of the country's descent into hell deliberately, to romanticize his death, and to trash-talk the current President, albeit in eloquent and lofty language and knowing allusions. In effect, they wrapped the murderous crimes of empire in the American flag.

McCain was a protégé of the founder of neo-conservatism, Senator Henry Scoop Jackson, a crazy servant of the British imperial agenda who constantly sought military confrontation with Russia. The British were so enamored of Jackson's views that they have dedicated an entire society of British intelligence spooks to him, the Henry Jackson Society. The former U.S. incarnations of this group were the Committee on the Present Danger and the Project for a New American Century. Leading members of both groups hastily retreated to the British mother ship after they led the U.S. mobilization for the failed and disastrous Iraq War. Former MI6 head Sir Richard Dearlove, who has shepherded the Christopher Steele and other British aspects of the coup against Donald Trump, is a leading member of this group.

Funding for McCain's political adventures came from his second wife, whose brewing company fortune was completely mixed up in the Arizona mob and mob funding during its earlier years.

With respect to McCain's activities, Max Blumenthal characterized them accurately in an August 27 *Consortium News* article: "McCain did not simply thunder for every major intervention in the post-Cold War era from the Senate floor. . . . He was uniquely ruthless when it comes to advancing imperial goals, barnstorming from one conflict zone to another to personally recruit far right fanatics as American proxies. In Libya and Syria, he cultivated affiliates of Al-Qaeda as allies, and in Ukraine, McCain recruited actual sig-heiling neo-Nazis."

Following the NATO-orchestrated murder of Libya's leader, McCain tweeted: "Qaddafi on his way out, Bashar

Al Assad is next." He backed the installation of the terrorist Muslim Brotherhood to govern Egypt, another failed and insane project. More than $5.6 trillion was spent chasing John McCain's idyll of democracy in Southwest Asia. Six thousand seven hundred Americans died, more than 50,000 were wounded, entire countries were reduced to rubble with accompanying genocide against their populations, and the largest mass human migration ever was sent into Europe, resembling something akin to the desperate mass flights of the Middle Ages.

It is these horrific actions by McCain, not the myth peddled at his funeral, which are the source of the conflict between Trump and John McCain, and between Trump and George Bush and Barack Obama. Trump promised to end the imperial policy of endless religious and population wars and Wall Street bailouts, and the voters responded resoundingly by electing him President.

The Manafort and Cohen Convictions

The media posited that these two convictions, one by trial, one by plea, gave Robert Mueller newfound credibility and "momentum" at a moment when both were dissipating extremely rapidly. This claim, like the others we have examined here, has no relation to reality.

Mueller's problem is that his entire investiga-

White House/Pete Souza
John Brennan

U.S. Government
Peter Strzok

tion has been revealed to be permeated with illegality and based on concepts of dubious constitutionality. As the result of investigations by Congress, we know that as of December 2015, British intelligence agencies were frantically signaling their fears about Donald Trump to Obama Administration intelligence officials, primarily the CIA of John Brennan. The British were demanding that Trump be taken out by any means necessary because he was "soft on Russia." They were demanding that Trump be taken out by criminalizing the idea for which the American people ultimately voted, that of having a rational relationship, rather than war, between the U.S. and Russia.

We now know that by early spring 2016, Brennan was operating out of the CIA with a taskforce investigating Trump based on British "leads," despite multiple legal prohibitions against precisely such domestic activity by the CIA. That task force included Peter Strzok, the now-fired FBI agent who said he would do anything to prevent Trump's election. This operation included sending informants to plant fabricated evidence on peripheral figures in the Trump campaign, including George Papadopoulos and Carter Page. The fake evidence suggested that Trump was using Russian obtained "dirt" against Hillary Clinton.

The evidence planting

operations, mostly conducted on British soil, were designed to back up the bogus and otherwise evidence-free and indefensible dossier authored by MI6's Christopher Steele—a dossier paid for by the Clinton campaign and promoted by the Department of State, Department of Justice, the FBI, and selected reporters. The dirty British Steele dossier claimed that Trump had been compromised by Putin. Based on this, Trump was targeted in a full-set counterintelligence investigation by the FBI, including surveillance of his campaign and anyone associated with it.

The goal of this surveillance was to put those who were around Trump under an investigative microscope stretching back years, to find any crime or misdeed for which they could be prosecuted. That is the illegal and unconstitutional backdrop to everything Robert Mueller has produced thus far. Nothing produced by Mueller has shown Trump to be a puppet of Putin as claimed by the British, the Clinton campaign, and the national news media. Nonetheless, the entire episode has damaged relations between the U.S. and Russia and between the U.S. and China, which was the British strategic goal in the first instance, continuing the dive into a new form of head-to-head confrontation between nuclear powers, bearing no comparison to the Cold War of the 20th Century.

Paul Manafort was hired to handle delegate selection at the Republican National Convention and then brought on as campaign manager. He worked for Trump for six months total until his legal problems became known and he resigned. He was charged by Mueller with tax, Foreign Agents Registration Act, and bank fraud offenses for his lobbying activities on behalf of the deposed government of Ukraine. That government was overthrown in a coup in which John McCain played a critical role, a coup which empowered outright neo-Nazis.

Christopher Steele, British intelligence, and the U.S. State Department also played major roles in the Ukraine regime change operation. Manafort was targeted by both Ukrainian and British intelligence because he, in effect, backed the perceived Russian side in the coup. For this, he was being investigated by the Obama Justice Department well prior to any campaign association with Donald Trump. Mueller simply adjusted the focus of this already political investigation, a focus aimed at turning Manafort into an asset against Trump by means of the terror of potential prison sentences numbering in the hundreds of years as the result of overcharged and duplicative indictments.

Michael Cohen, who worked with Trump as a lawyer, also had his share of prior legal problems, primarily related to taxes concerning his taxi medallion business in New York City. For months, the mainstream media has featured the claims of porn star Stormy Daniels claiming a one-night stand with the future President, ten years ago, as if the nation could draw some lesson from Daniels about public virtue. Cohen apparently arranged to pay off Daniels and another woman concerning their allegations about sex with the President. Among other suspicious dealings, Cohen made audio recordings of conversations with his client, Donald Trump, during the campaign, a complete and total violation of legal ethics which would independently cost him his law license. For many months prior to his plea deal, Cohen had been a target of intense investigative interest based on his tax problems.

In recent months, Cohen has repeatedly signaled that he was willing to betray the President and say whatever prosecutors in the Southern District of New York wanted him to say about Donald Trump in order to avoid jail. The problem is that prosecutors thought Cohen an obvious desperate liar and were not buying. Ultimately, the deal which Cohen struck has him claiming that candidate Trump asked him to pay hush money to the women, resulting in Federal Election Campaign Act violations. This is what the Justice Department claimed against John Edwards in a widely ridiculed and failed prosecution. It is exactly the type of claim by which the British and our Establishment impeached Bill Clinton.

Cohen hired long-time Clinton operative Lanny Davis to represent him in recent months and to make a deal. Following his plea, Davis claimed that Cohen had two made-up morsels to offer Mueller, in return for a reduced sentence: a claim that Trump knew about the June 2016 Trump Tower meeting with a Russian lawyer, and a claim that Cohen knew about Russian hacking of Hillary Clinton's emails. Davis has since admitted that both these claims were totally false and has had to walk them back publicly.

So, if you are tempted by the media to think that either of these "convictions" is germane to the President's fitness for office, or Robert Mueller's credibility, please, seek medical attention. The madness which now infects much of official Washington may have claimed you.

ZEPP-LAROUCHE WEBCAST

In Collaboration with China, Africa Will Be a Powerhouse of the Future

This is the edited transcript of the Schiller Institutes' September 6, 2018 New Paradigm interview with the founder of the Schiller Institutes, Helga Zepp-LaRouche, by Harley Schlanger. A video *of the webcast is available.*

Harley Schlanger: Hello! I'm Harley Schlanger from the Schiller Institute. Welcome to our weekly strategic international update, featuring our founder and President, Helga Zepp-LaRouche.

It's really quite extraordinary how rapidly developments are taking place, both in terms of the consolidation of the New Paradigm around the New Silk Road, but also especially around the escalation that's being conducted by the London-linked geopolitical networks that are out to stop that New Paradigm.

In the last few days, we've seen the release of Bob Woodward's new fictional book, called *Fear: Trump in the White House*. And there is the Sept. 5 op-ed in the *New York Times*, supposedly by a top official in the Trump Administration, about an internal resistance movement in the White House, and a number of other things we'll get to in the course of this program today. Helga, it's clear from these developments that there is a fear that everything that's been thrown at Trump so far with Russiagate is not going to succeed, but they're going for the kill anyway, aren't they?

Helga Zepp-LaRouche: I think Trump's tweet in answering all of this is absolutely right, that he is winning. Now, to just look at what is happening: The Woodward book has already been refuted by both White House Chief of Staff John Kelly and Secretary of Defense James Mattis, both of whom are quoted in the book, and both of whom have said that what is said there is complete fraud.

Then there is the *New York Times* publishing an anonymous op-ed saying that there are many people in the administration working to undo the worst inclinations of Trump. This is not news. We have said from Day One that the neo-cons in the Trump Administration were working on every level to sabotage the policies of Trump, and in many cases, the reason Trump has not made the kind of progress he could have made, is due to these moles and this cabal.

So this is a typical operation, much like what was done in Italy many years ago, called "Operation Clean Hands." It targetted corruption that was part of the postwar Italian political system—you do me a favor and I do you one—which was the Italian system. At a certain point, when the same forces now behind this present operation against Trump decided to dismantle all existing parties in Italy, they published everything. It's not that these crimes were something new. A typical method of the British and other similar secret service organizations is to blow up their own operations when they want to go for maximum destabilization.

The publication of the Woodward book combined with the *New York Times* article is supposed to induce a paranoid response from Trump about who he can trust and who not (as if he were not already dealing with exactly that sort of problem). It was also designed to get people all worked up and insecure about Trump winning.

This is not just an isolated set of events in the United States. At the same time, Prime Minister Theresa May went to the British Parliament, claiming the British government has proof that the Skripal assassination attempt, and the subsequent attempt on two other individuals in England, is now proven to have been carried out by two Russian GRU [military intelligence] agents. She claimed that they arrived in England on March 3 and then went to try to kill Skripal. Afterward returning to a hotel in London—and Novichok was found in this very hotel. Then, according to May, they took a plane and went back to Russia.

This is ridiculous. British government officials say that they don't even know the names of the two individuals, yet they say that they know that these two people are GRU agents. In the UN Security Council meeting called by Great Britain, the Russian ambassador refuted the British claims, emphasizing that there is not one single shred of evidence against Russia and that Russia has not been involved in any part of the investigation and Russia completely rejects it.

UK Parliament

Prime Minister Theresa May tells Parliament, without any evidence, that her government has proof that the Russians did it.

Planned False-Flag Chemical Attack in Syria

This goes hand-in-hand with the ongoing danger of a false flag operation in Idlib, Syria. Almost all of the remaining al-Qaeda and ISIS terrorists assembled in Idlib, after all the other territories in Syria were taken back by the government. Now an offensive against those terrorists has begun by the Syrian armed forces, with some Russian support. The Russians had earlier presented proof, including to the Organization for the Prohibition of Chemical Weapons (OPCW), that the terrorist-supporting White Helmets and another British private security firm were involved in producing false evidence, that chemical agents were being shipped to two villages near Idlib. Teams are ready to film the suffering of the victims. The Russian government said they have proof that this is a planned fake-news event, a fabricated story.

The British government charged instead that it is the Syrian government that is planning to use chemical weapons in their attack on Idlib.

Unfortunately, Secretary of State Mike Pompeo and National Security Advisor John Bolton both accused Syrian President Bashar al-Assad and warned him that if he were to move against Idlib, then this would have terrible consequences. It took former Senator Ron Paul to say that Americans should remind themselves that the people now sitting in Idlib, at the least the terrorist element, are the same forces that carried out the 9/11 attacks in the United States, and asked whether anybody wanted to have them replace Assad?

Trump Could Release All FISA Documents

This is wild, completely wild. The aim of all these operations is to get the necessary increase in the vote for Democrats, so that the Democrats could go for an impeachment, counting on some treasonous Republicans joining them in this effort. This is absolutely dangerous. I appeal to everyone to not fall for this trap—all the accusations against Trump have been fabricated. I'm very happy that the Freedom Caucus will have a press conference today, demanding that Trump release all the documents relating to the FBI requests to the FISA Court for surveillance, and all the notes exchanged by Bruce Ohr with respect to his relationship with Christopher Steele, and everything else.

National Security

Republican lawmakers will review classified information on FBI source Thursday, White House says

House Intelligence Committee Chairman Devin Nunes (R-Calif.), right, speaks with Freedom Caucus Chairman Mark Meadows (R-N.C.) in Washington on Sunday. (Erin Schaff/For The Washington Post)

By **Karoun Demirjian** and **Matt Zapotosky**
May 22

Just two Republican lawmakers will be allowed to review classified information about a confidential FBI source who aided the investigation into the Trump campaign at a meeting Thursday with Justice Department

That, in a certain sense, is the "nuclear option," because Trump could turn the tables completely by publishing all of the documents and letting the people of the United States decide who are the criminals in this whole story, and who are not.

Schlanger: One element of the *New York Times* op-ed that I thought was a kind of marker of the defensiveness of this faction, was the phrase, "This isn't the work of the so-called deep state." What does that describe? It describes operatives inside the White House operating against President Trump's agenda, which, of course, is what Trump has said from the beginning is the problem he has. And it's not just the Democrats, but people in the Republican Party as well.

Last week I was in the United States, and had the misfortune of watching American television. It was nonstop coverage of the McCain funeral, presenting Sen. John McCain as the great hero, the bipartisan figure, the person who could bridge the divide. Not a single mention of McCain's commitment to war, his pushing of the lies concerning Iraq. Remember, McCain had a role to play in the initial Russiagate case,

in which he was one of the first people, I think the first Senator, to get a copy of the Christopher Steele dossier.

We now see the neo-cons and the neo-liberals coming together, moving to get rid of Trump. There have been two very important commentaries in the last few days pointing to the danger of war if they succeed. Helga, you're very familiar with Willy Wimmer, a former top defense official in Germany, and also Paul Craig Roberts. Why don't you give us a report on what they had to say?

Former Officials Warn of Collusion with British

Zepp-LaRouche: I find it very significant that two former government officials have spoken out. Willy Wimmer was the German deputy defense minister in the Helmut Kohl era, and Paul Craig Roberts had a similar post in the U.S. Treasury in the Reagan Administration. We have very interesting insights from two officials who come from an earlier era—based on completely different axioms, a completely different paradigm.

Paul Craig Roberts said that history demonstrates that these almost unbelievable provocations, now coming from the neo-con and British Empire apparatus, always lead to war. Patriots in Russia, he said, are now putting pressure on Putin, saying that he is too patient—this despite the fact that Russia, with its news weapons systems, probably has the capability to annihilate much of the West without much damage being suffered by Russia. Nevertheless, Putin doesn't want to risk nuclear war—the consequences are unknown, and it would lead to enormous unprecedented destruction.

Roberts encourages Putin to be more forceful and say what will happen to the West if it comes to war. That is very useful, because I think people should really be aware of this—we are talking about consequences that potentially mean the nuclear extinction of civilization.

I'm very happy that Willy Wimmer warned of the danger of what would happen if Republicans were to join the Democrats for the impeachment of President Trump. He said that people should remember how absolutely tense the situation was in the Presidential election in 2016. If Trump had lost and people thought that there had been vote fraud, the whole situation could have erupted in a civil war. Wimmer further says that the great danger is, indeed, World War III—2018 may be the last year in which we have peace in Europe.

This is very important. I urge people to read these two articles. They are the total opposite of the mainstream media. Wimmer also says, if you listen to the commentaries on McCain's death, you can see where the hearts of the European heads of government are, namely on the side of the war faction, with Obama and Hillary Clinton, that with the kinds of things they are saying, we would be right back on the war track should the drive for Trump's impeachment succeed.

Xinhua/Ju Peng

Chinese President Xi Jinping and South African President Cyril Ramaphosa, co-chairs of the Forum on China-Africa Cooperation (FOCAC), and heads of delegations of 53 other African members of the FOCAC, arrive at the venue of the roundtable meeting of the 2018 FOCAC Beijing Summit, at the Great Hall of the People in Beijing, Sept. 4.

I think people should not take this lightly, just because war is not on the minds of many people. The British Empire is absolutely determined to press ahead. Wimmer calls it the "deep state." We know it's actually the collusion between what some call the "deep state" in the United States and British intelligence and the British government in the British Empire.

This is the time to really defeat this. The first step would be to publish all the materials on this affair. It is very important for Americans to vote, and to organize others to vote for the candidates who have been loyal to Trump and for whom Trump has campaigned, rather than holding back because Trump, or some of these candidates, are not perfect on all matters. We need to intervene with our programmatic ideas. Right now, the world is on the verge of a financial crash. The danger of a massive financial blowout is now looming. Trichet, the former President of the European Central Bank, said we could have a blowout much worse than 2008 *at any minute*; look at the reverse carry trade in the emerging markets; we're sitting on a global powder keg.

So now is the time to mobilize. Sign and circulate our petition for the United States, Russia, China, and India, and possibly Japan, to organize a New Bretton Woods conference. Only if we change the agenda completely can this situation be turned around.

Forum on China-Africa Cooperation

Schlanger: Let me emphasize the war danger one more time. The charges in the Skripal affair and the possible false-flag chemical attack in Idlib province are types of maneuvers the British Empire forces have done before. Why are they trying again? Why is the Skripal case reemerging? Because they're driving for war, and as Wimmer and Paul Craig Roberts said, that's their only option, their only alternative.

The better alternative for mankind was clearly demonstrated in a conference in Beijing, which we talked about last week. The summit of the Forum on China-Africa Cooperation (FOCAC) has now taken place. Helga, I would say it was quite an amazing success. What do you have on the final outcome of this conference?

Zepp-LaRouche: In my humble opinion, the FOCAC conference will go down in history as the official ending of colonialism—because of the kinds of agreements between China and the nations of Africa. There were almost 50 African heads of state attending. Only five heads of state did not go, for one or another reason—they sent their prime ministers instead. There was such a high-level agreement between China and the African continent, and China and individual countries, that I think what Cyril Ramaphosa, the President of South Africa said, puts it in a nutshell: He said, the "golden age of China-African relations has begun." And he said that the accusation that China is luring the African nations into a debt trap is completely ludicrous, the notion that China is pushing a new neocolonialism is ridiculous.

Africa is now free, and African nations can choose which partners are in their best interests.

This is a completely new tone. And one has to also note the irony that the debt trap argument is coming from the old colonialist forces and the media of those colonial powers that continued colonial looting of Africa for centuries. Those are the voices now freaking out about Chinese "neocolonialism." No one in Africa thinks this is true. Every single head of state who spoke at the FOCAC conference praised the fact that it was with Chinese help that their respective countries now have the chance to develop, in a very short period of time, into modern countries with a good income for their general populations—the exact and total opposite of colonialism.

I think this FOCAC conference was a watershed. It will open up even more possibilities for other countries to join in, as we see such a possibility developing in Italy. Italy is a good exception to the stupidity rampant in Europe. Michele Geraci, Italy's Undersecretary of State for Economic Development, attended this FOCAC conference with the China task force he helped develop for the Italian government. Italy is one shining example of a Western country saying, let's join hands with China, to develop Africa. Others instead say they have to have a counterplan. I think it's stupid. We should just really realize that this is a world-historical opportunity to bring the world into a new paradigm of cooperation— people and nations should join rather than sticking to old, geopolitical positions which are untenable anyway.

This FOCAC conference is extremely good. Many bilateral deals were made between Egypt and China. China will invest massively in energy development in Egypt. Similarly, deals were struck between China and Nigeria, China and South Africa, and with many other countries. So, I think this is really the beginning, as Ramaphosa said, the beginning of a new "golden age."

A Turning Point in History

All the aspirations of all those countries, which were rejected for such a long time, are now on a positive and good footing. People should really follow these events. Read the African newspapers—they're full of praise.

The editor of the German weekly newspaper *Die Zeit* wrote about the FOCAC meeting that it was the colonizer and the colonized, and then he went on to say, "The British at least brought infrastructure to India!" [laughs] This is really funny—it shows you, first of all, whose song he is singing, namely that of the British Empire. Just ask the Indians what they think about what British marauders did for them. Listen to this very important speech given by an Indian Member of Parliament, Dr. Shashi Tharoor—actually in Britain—blasting the crimes of the British Empire against India. The two Opium Wars against China, what all the colonialist powers did in Africa has not been forgotten.

This is liberation: This is really a turning point in history. The news media in the United States did not publish one single word about this summit. In Germany, coverage was very negative for the most part. There was only one objective TV report about it, which one has to note as an exception.

Form your own opinion: World-historical changes are taking place, for the good and for the better. Western Europe and the United States should join this—it is a very happy potential for all of humanity.

China Developing, not 'Debt-Trapping' the World

Schlanger: To help form your opinion on this, you can go to the Schiller Institute's website to get the report that we've written on the Belt and Road Initiative in Africa, and also a new paper that we've just posted, refuting the argument about the so-called "debt trap." While we're speaking of infrastructure, let me mention a new report put out by the OECD on the deficit in infrastructure in the advanced sector countries. I think they're talking about somewhere between $80 and $90 trillion that will be needed by 2030. What did they conclude?

Zepp-LaRouche: The report says that $71 trillion in investment is needed, but then a banking analyst said, no, it's $94 trillion. Thirty million km of roads need to be repaired or built—this is 40 times the round trip from the Earth to the Moon. And there are 1.1 billion people without electricity and 1.5 billion have no access to fresh water.

This has to be remedied. At the FOCAC meeting in Beijing, it became clear that there is a complete coherence between China's Belt and Road Initiative; the UN Agenda 2030 that aims at eradicating poverty, which agenda was heavily influenced in the recent period by China; and the African Union's Agenda 2063—the 50-year perspective Africa gave itself in 2013, when it released this plan. It is a very, very ambitious plan.

All the African leaders stressed that this is not anybody else's wish, this is Africa's wish—that Africa should become a fully modernized continent, leapfrogging many technologies to world-class, state-of-the-art ones, eradicating poverty, transforming their societies into ones of good, middle-class income. Africa is now on that road to success. I find it, again, absolutely unbelievable that you have something accomplished which everybody said they wanted, including lefties—those who had expressed grave concern for the people of the third world—but they are not yet joyfully joining in, in spreading the knowledge of this summit throughout Europe and the United States. The truth is that they don't care! Instead, many of them have sided with the FBI and the CIA and the Department of Justice against Trump.

There's something wrong with the thinking of such people, something has happened to all of them.

Let me challenge you, our audience: Join the Schiller Institute, help us spread the information about China and Africa. Make sure that the mobilization for the midterm elections in the United States is on the right path. Because, as Willy Wimmer correctly says, the fate of the world hangs on those midterm elections.

North Korea and the Singapore Model

Schlanger: One perfect example—and this will be the final point we get to today—is North Korea. The opponents of Trump keep saying, "There's no change, it's not going to work." You, Helga, have laid out very beautifully the idea of the "Singapore model" representing a new option for humanity. We have the report from Kim Jong-un today that he is completely committed to denuclearization during the time period Trump is in office. So again, Helga, we see the difference between a positive approach, the Singapore model, and those clinging to the same old paradigm of war, regime change and chaos.

Zepp-LaRouche: Well, yes. And then in a few days, maybe less than two weeks, President Moon Jae-in of South Korea will go to Pyongyang and will discuss with Kim Jong-un denuclearization and cooperation. This is also very, very important to keep in

Xinhua/Inter-Korean Summit Press Corps

South Korean President Moon Jae-in (right) and North Korean Leader Kim Jong-un, at the border village of Panmunjom, rekindle hope of a lasting peace on the Korean Peninsula, April 27, 2018.

mind. The Singapore model demonstrates that you can turn every crisis into its opposite, by deciding to concentrate on the interest of the other—win-win cooperation—and uplift the whole discussion to a New Paradigm.

That all can happen. We have so many positive developments—the transformation of Africa, the resolution of the Korea conflict—there is much reason to be optimistic about defeating the British Empire's antics in Syria, provocations in the Skripal poisoning case, and its impeachment drive to unseat President Trump. All they have to offer is negativity. And I think people should not allow themselves to be drawn into that. Mobilize right now: It's probably the most important time of our lives to do so.

Schlanger: Anything else you want to add, Helga?

Zepp-LaRouche: No. I think that is it.

Schlanger: OK! We covered a lot. And we'll be back next week, with next week's Schiller Institute webcast. Thank you for joining us.

S. Mahmud Ali:
Lyndon and Helga LaRouche, Prophets of the New Silk Road

by S. Mahmud Ali

S. Mahmud Ali

This is an edited extract of a chapter, titled "America's Foundational Contributions to China's Belt & Road Initiative," posted by the author, S. Mahmud Ali, on LinkedIn, from his forthcoming book, China's Belt and Road Vision: Geo-Economics and Geopolitics, *to be published by Springer in 2019. It is published here by permission of the author. Ali is an Associate Fellow at the Institute of China Studies, University of Malaya, and author of several books on the Asia-Pacific region.*

Aug. 26—Western BRI [Belt and Road Initiative] discourse, especially commentary by U.S. strategic analysts and even cabinet-level leaders, not to speak of responsible officials making policy-statements or drafting high-level executive- and legislative branch documents, and contributing to the rapidly growing China-focused academic literature have, over the past five years since Xi Jinping proclaimed his BRI vision, made clear their disdain for the initiative, and underscored their suspicions that Beijing's BRI vision is, in fact, a geopolitical stratagem aimed at non-violently supplanting America at the core of the post-Soviet international security system, dressed up as an innocuous geo-economic plan to gird the planet with Chinese-designed infrastructure, trade and regulatory norms with all roads leading to Beijing.

Repeated *ad nauseam*, not only by U.S. officials, media-observers and academic researchers, this view has become the mainstream not only in the U.S.A., but also in U.S.-allied and -aligned states, especially across Western Europe, Japan, India and Australia. Coincidentally, the latter three, led by the U.S.A., have recently revived their 2007-vintage Quadrilateral Initiative, or the Quad, to deter feared Chinese aggression across the newly-proclaimed Indo-Pacific stretching, in the words of the recently retired Commander of the U.S. Pacific Command, now renamed the U.S. Indo-Pacific Command, "from Hollywood to Bollywood." Naval drills, policy coordination and official remarks by the leaders of the four states make clear their collective determination to stop any Chinese attempts or even intent—repeatedly denied by Beijing—to erode American and allied force-projection capabilities all along China's periphery, defeat the PLA in combat if China crosses certain "red lines," and extend America's systemic primacy into the indefinite future.

It is in this context that the BRI has been viewed by leaders, legislators and their advisors in these capitals, although their counterparts from at least 68 countries in Asia, Europe, Africa, Latin America and Oceania appear to have voluntarily joined China in benefiting from the BRI. This notable dichotomy, while clear and widely un-

Xinhua/Wang Ye

Chinese President Xi Jinping announcing the New Silk Road policy at the Nazarbayev University in Astana, Kazakhstan, Sept. 7, 2013.

Lyndon LaRouche and Helga Zepp-LaRouche, Leesburg, Virginia, 1986.

seminal construct of the "world island," its two-tiered "peripheries" and the need to dominate this territory or, at least prevent it from falling to hostile hands, shaped Western strategic thinking for over a century. This motivation acquired added salience following the Soviet collapse and the advent of U.S. primacy which began confronting challenges in the early 21st Century.[2] While official and semi-official analyses viewed the possible rise of "near-peer rivals" in Eurasia, namely Russia and China, Western thinkers operating outside state-funded national security establishments envisioned a non-competitive, indeed collaborative, vision of the future.

One of them, the U.S. politician and co-founder, with his wife Helga LaRouche, of the Washington-based Schiller Institute, Lyndon LaRouche, promoted such a vision, with some success in influencing segments of trans-Atlantic opinion.[3] In October 1988, LaRouche briefed the media in

derstood, does not explain the BRI's historical evolution. The BRI's terrestrial component, the Silk Road Economic Belt, an overland network of roads, railways, airports, transport hubs, fibre-optic cables, oil and gas pipelines, and coordinated regulatory frameworks easing and optimizing their trans-Eurasian utilization, in fact, originated in America, with U.S. visionaries envisaging, promoting and advancing the cause of a united Euro-Asian economic space, as early as the late 1980s, before politicians and their assorted advisers had begun considering the possibility of the collapse of the Soviet Union, or the end of the Cold War. It was that American intellectual spark, nurtured by a few far-sighted men and women, which illuminated the new world of possibilities. Without it, and direct intervention by governments and multilateral agencies based in America and its allies, there would probably be no BRI today.

American Prophets Imagine a New Silk Road

Western imagery of Eurasia and imagination of Asia played a significant role in creating a European collective and ideational identity in opposition to the non-European-inhabited continental landmass stretching away eastward. Early in the 20th Century, the eminent British geopolitician, Halford Mackinder, posited, "European civilization is, in a very real sense, the outcome of the secular struggle against Asiatic invasion."[1] His

2. "The U.S. Grand Strategy and the Eurasian Heartland in the 21st Century," Emre Iseri. *Geopolitics,* Vol. 14, Issue 1, February 2009, pp. 26-46; "From Competition to Compatibility: Striking a Eurasian Balance in EU-Russia Relations," Tony van der Togt, Francesco Montesano, and Iaroslav Kozak. Clingendael Institute, The Hague, Oct. 2015.
3. Friedrich von Schiller's plays and romantic poetry contributed to shaping post-revolutionary European thought. His *Ode to Joy*, which praised freedom, unity and the brotherhood of all mankind in a period that had divided and frozen society into an arbitrary stratification, was set to music by Beethoven in his Ninth Symphony. That symphony is now celebrated as the European Union's collective anthem. C. Rabitz (2009). Friedrich Schiller's works have withstood the trials of revolution. *DW,* Bonn, Nov. 10, 2009.

EIRNS/Dean Andromidas

Lyndon LaRouche forecasts the fall of the Soviet Union and reunification of Germany in a speech in West Berlin, Oct. 22, 1988.

1. "The Geographical Pivot of History," Halford Mackinder. *The Geographic Journal,* 1904. 23:422.

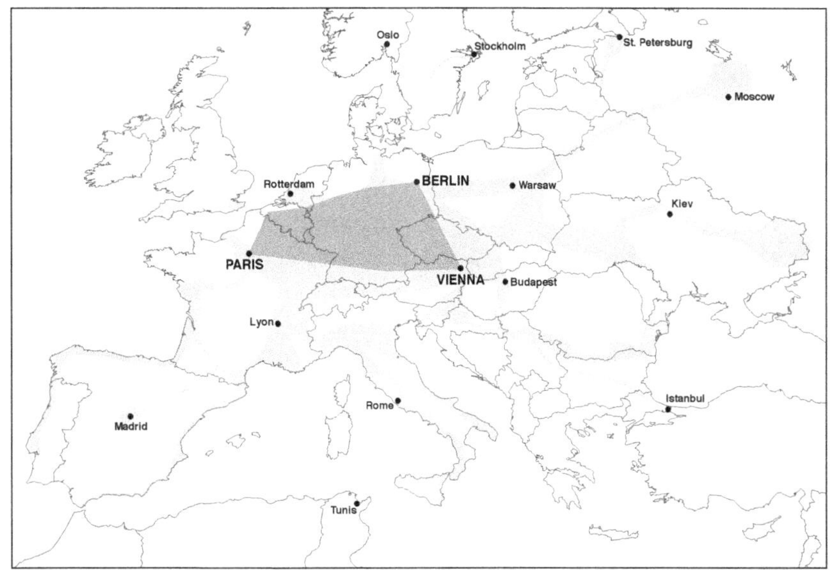

Schiller Institute

LaRouche's concept of the European Productive Triangle Paris-Berlin-Vienna, 1988-90.

West Berlin on "U.S. Policy Toward the Reunification of Germany," prophesying the collapse of COMECON economies, and urging food-support to Poland so that a "majority of Germans on both sides" desired reunification. In December, he assigned a group of Schiller Institute specialists to examine prospects for establishing a Paris-Berlin-Vienna "productive triangle." In January 1990, the Schiller Institute published LaRouche's book on a proposed 320,000 square-kilometer European economic area comprising a population of 92 million concentrated in 10 large industrial areas, from which he envisaged infrastructural corridors, linked with high-speed railways, radiating in all directions, "providing a basis for upgrading living standards" across Eurasia.[4]

At the Schiller Institute's March 1991 "Infrastructure for a Free Europe" conference in Berlin, LaRouche's paper—as he was a prisoner in America since January 1989—urging the construction of "a sphere of cooperation for mutual benefit among sovereign states" of Europe and Asia, was read out to over 100 participants from 17 countries. In October 1991, at the first All-European Conference on Transport in Prague, the Schiller Institute staff distributed literature describing energy-and-technology-intensive economic corridors radiating from Europe's "productive triangle." In No-

vember, 400 delegates from almost three-dozen countries, including former Soviet republics, gathered at the Schiller Institute's Berlin conference on "The Productive Triangle: Cornerstone of an All-Eurasian Program of Eurasian Development."

In 1992, Schiller Institute economists detailed the "spiral arms" or economic/infrastructure corridors radiating from the "productive triangle," claiming resonances in Beijing's "Eurasian Land-Bridge" initiatives as the Chinese-Kazakh rail connectivity became operational in June 1992. This made it possible for the first time to travel 11,000 km from China's Yellow Sea port of Lianyungang across Eurasia to Rotterdam.[5] LaRouche's political action committee and the Schiller Institute mounted a privately funded campaign aimed at persuading the American political mainstream to abandon its "policy of antagonism towards China, and Russia," and embrace Eurasian economic integration instead.[6] This proved to be a particularly complex undertaking.

In late 1993, the European Union championed Jacques Delors' eponymous "Delors Plan" to extend Western Europe's high-speed railway network into

5. "From Productive Triangle to Eurasian Land-Bridge." Schiller Institute. Undated. Accessed Jan. 23, 2018.
6. "The U.S. Joins the New Silk Road: A Hamiltonian Vision for an Economic Renaissance." LaRouche Political Action Committee. Leesburg, VA, 2018, pp. 1-5. Accessed May 19, 2018.

EIRNS/Christopher Lewis

Lyndon LaRouche addresses a Schiller Institute conference, focused on the New Silk Road development policy, Eltville, Germany, Nov. 12, 1994.

---

4. "The Productive Triangle: Locomotive for the World Economy," Lyndon LaRouche. Schiller Institute, West Berlin, 1990. (in German)

EIRNS

Symposium on Economic Development Along the New Euro-Asia Continental Bridge, Beijing, China, May 7-9, 1996.

former Soviet-bloc Central and Eastern European countries, starting with a Berlin-Warsaw section, and raising the prospects for the eventual fashioning of a "continental bridge" linking Europe to ports in Asian Russia and, later, China. Unlike the Schiller Institute's theoretical proposition, the EU's more pragmatic plan excluded the war-torn Balkans. In December 1994, the recently freed Lyndon LaRouche presided over the Schiller Institute's conference on "Global Economic Recovery and the Cultural Renaissance" in Eltville, Germany, leading a seminar on Eurasian development corridors attended by leading figures from China, Russia, Ukraine and Eastern Europe.

This led, on May 7-9, 1996, to the UNDP [United Nations Development Programme], the UN Department for Development Support and Management Services, the WBG [World Bank Group], EU Commission, ADB [Asian Development Bank] and other multilateral and international organizations helping the Chinese government to host a three-day "Symposium on Economic Development along New Euro-Asia Continental Bridge" in Beijing. More than 400 delegates representing governments, academia and businesses discussed the status of socio-economic development across Eurasia,

"thereby, laying the groundwork for a new continental bridge to cover a vast area of the Eurasian continent."[7] In addition to ministerial-level officials from China and other participating states, and non-governmental contributors to the Eurasian economic-infrastructural integration discourse, co-founder of the Schiller Institute Helga Zepp-LaRouche, addressed the gathering, focusing on "Building the Silk Road Land-Bridge: The Basis for the Mutual Security Interests of Asia and Europe."

Coincidentally, around this time, Iran and Turkmenistan announced the opening of the Mashhad-Ashgabat railway line, enabling direct rail-transport from the Persian Gulf to Central Asia and further east and west, potentially knitting much of the southern half of Eurasia into a cohesive transport network. In January 1997, Lyndon LaRouche addressed a Washington conference, urging the Clinton Administration to sponsor a "New Bretton Woods system," reorganizing the world economy to prevent disruptive boombust cycles, and recognize the global merit of the

---

7. "Symposium on Economic Development along New Euro-Asia Continental Bridge Opens in Beijing." UN Information Office, New York, May 9, 1996.

Schiller Institute/Mary Burdman

Helga Zepp-LaRouche addresses professors and students in Beijing, China, May, 1986.

"Eurasian Land-Bridge" program. Reinforcing and explaining her husband's persistent thematic refrain, Helga Zepp-LaRouche published a commentary titled, "Eurasian Land-Bridge: A New Era for Mankind," which was widely circulated across the Atlantic by the Schiller Institute.[8] In October-November 1997, she presented a paper on "Principles of Foreign Policy in the Coming Era of the New Eurasian Land-Bridge" at a conference themed, "Asia-Europe Economic and Trade Relations in the 21st Century and the 2nd Eurasian Bridge," hosted by Beijing with multilateral financial assistance. By then, railway connectivity between coastal China, Central Asia and Russia was a reality; Europe beckoned.[9]

A year-and-a-half later, in July 1999, the Schiller Institute's India representative, Ramtanu Maitra, convened an academic seminar in Delhi with Russian, Chinese, and Indian scholars discussing triangular collaboration across Eurasia. R.B. Ryabkov, Chairman of the Russian Academy of Sciences Institute of Oriental Studies, Ma Jiali, a professor at the Chinese Institute for Contemporary International Relations (CICIR), and Devendra Kaushik, Head of the School of International Studies at Jawaharlal Nehru University in Delhi, discussed challenges and prospects. With Ryabkov presiding, the scholars established a "Triangular Association" with the goal of promoting Indo-Russian-Chinese cooperation in forging a shared vision of Eurasia's post-Cold War future of peace, progress and prosperity. The effort failed for a combination of distractions and difficulties: fallout from the "Asian Economic Crisis," the September 2001 al-Qaeda attacks on New York City and Wash-

EIRNS/Stuart Lewis

Lyndon LaRouche and Helga Zepp-LaRouche on the occasion of her 65th birthday, Round Hill, Virginia, Aug. 25, 2013.

ington and America's subsequent "Global War on Terrorism," wars in Afghanistan and Iraq, and then, the Great Recession.[10] Nonetheless, seeds had been sown in the febrile post-Cold War intellectual hotbeds. Ideas analyzed at the Schiller Institute's many conferences and events began gelling into policy-frameworks in early 21st century.

The LaRouches were not the only American visionaries imagining a new, post-Cold War, inter-connected Eurasian future. The Schiller Institute's protracted endeavors eventually percolated into U.S. academia. S. Frederick Starr, a Johns Hopkins University scholar specializing in Central Asian studies, presided over a conference themed "Partnership, Trade and Development in Greater Central Asia" in Kabul, Afghanistan, in April 2006, amidst the U.S.-led counter-Taliban campaign raging across much of the country. A number of mostly Western specialists presented papers which were later edited into a volume titled, *The New Silk Roads: Transport and Trade in Greater Central Asia*, and published in 2007.[11] By this time, the U.S. Congress was already actively exploring legislative options supportive of the U.S. engagement with the region and regional cohesion, with a view to strengthening America's strategic influence and footprint there. So, the general concept of Eurasian transport-and-trade integration, with many separate but inter-connected points of origin, including scholarly American minds, came together early in the new century. Execution, dogged by practical, political, financial, regulatory and engineering challenges, was slow. Beijing's assumption of leadership, with much multilateral support, propelled the drive to forge the BRI.

---

8. "Eurasian Land-Bridge: A New Era for Mankind," Helga Zepp-LaRouche. *Executive Intelligence Review*, Vol. 24, No. 19, May 2, 1997, pp. 21-25.

9. "The New Asia-Europe Land Bridge: Current Situation and Future Prospects." Xu Shu, *Japan Railway and Transport Review*, Dec. 1997, pp. 30-33.

10. "The Alliance of India-Russia-China." A paper presented at Conference on "The 2nd American Revolution: Developing the Pacific and Ending the Grip of Empire," Ramtanu Maitra. Schiller Institute, Los Angeles, CA, Nov. 2, 2013.

11. *The New Silk Roads: Transport and Trade in Greater Central Asia.* S. Frederick Starr (ed.), Johns Hopkins University, Washington, DC, 2007.

Discovering Your True Enemy

by Stewart Battle

Inglorious Empire: What the British Did to India
Shashi Tharoor
London: C. Hurst & Co., March 2017
Paperback, 336 pages, $14.86

Sept. 8—How is it that we find ourselves at this current state of world affairs today? How have we let our once most prosperous and most optimistic nation fall into such a state of disrepair—and the noble goals for which we once stood turn to cynicism and corruption? What process, what *force*, has been responsible for this? One often hears the phrase: "people don't know their history." A true statement, indeed. But do those critics themselves actually know their history—know what has shaped our world today, or know what set our United States apart in all this, with the potential to fundamentally change the history of mankind? The answer to this, lies in understanding the most brutal, mass-murderous, and evil force in modern history: the British Empire.

Shashi Tharoor, Indian Parliamentarian, author, and former UN Under-Secretary-General, recently released a book that usefully exposes the bloody history of the British Empire—*Inglorious Empire: What the British Did to India*. Tharoor became somewhat of an Internet sensation a few years ago when he participated in a debate at Oxford on the subject of the British owing reparations to India for the 200 years of colonial rule. The response to his comments was so explosive and positive, including from many In-

dians (as well as Britons) who wished they knew more about this history, that Tharoor decided to elaborate his arguments in a more in-depth format, which became this book.

Inglorious Empire illustrates some key facets of the 200 years of crimes committed by the British in India and lays to shame the notion of a "benign" British Empire, as argued by many academics still today. This is a history rich with outright looting and pillaging, the complete destruction of India's economy, cultural and psychological brainwashing, sowing division and partitioning its territory with the creation of Pakistan, and the murder of *tens of millions* through a policy of intentional famine. India will never forget what the British did. As Tharoor says, before the British arrived India accounted for fully 25 percent of the world's economy. By the time the British left, India had been reduced to a mere three percent of the world's economy, while Britain had grown to rule a global empire.

However, despite this very useful exposé and discussion of the history of the British Empire, Tharoor's book fails in some very crucial ways. Most notably, Tharoor—like most today—understates and likely does not understand the true nature of the British Empire, and therefore seemingly misses the forest for the trees. While British rule in India was blatantly evil, it differs not at all in its genocidal effects from what the British continue to execute on a global scale in the form of today's Anglo-Dutch imperial system. One must recognize the *symptoms* of empire that Tharoor illustrates well in his book, but the actual *underly-*

CC/Chatham House
Dr. Shashi Tharoor

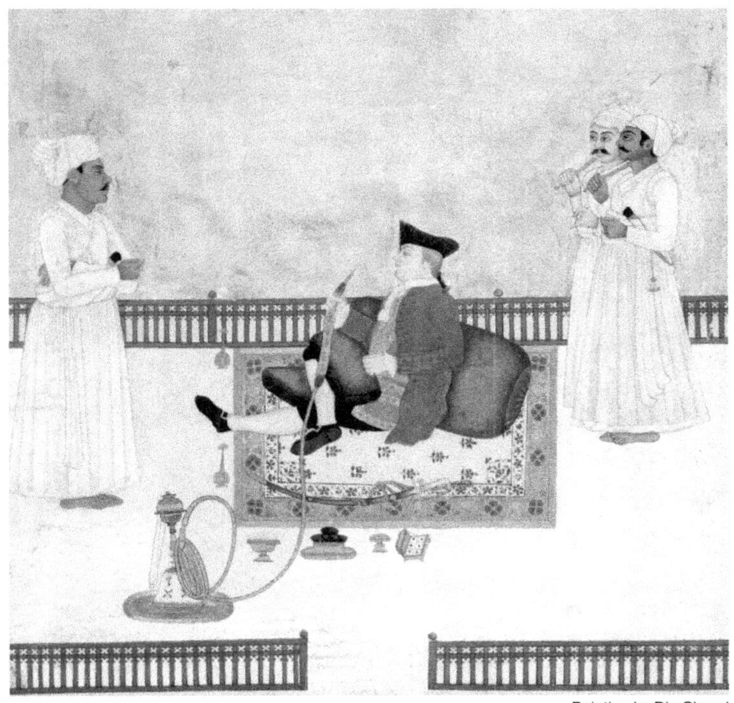

Depiction of an official of the British East India Company, ca. 1760.

ing principle of empire is a principle that continues unbroken today. That is the true history that Americans and others must understand now. In this light, I summarize here some of the most crucial aspects of Tharoor's book.

Economic Looting

The British East India Company was in India as early as the beginning of the 17th Century. It began to conquer different regions and bring them under its control in the mid-18th Century. As Tharoor points out, taxes on property soon averaged 80-90 percent of the rental value, making for a 328 percent increase in total land revenue within 30 years, in the case of Bengal—purely a looting scheme in which Indians were forced deeper and deeper into poverty while pockets were filled back in Britain. The story goes that if British tax collectors found a citizen to be delinquent on taxes, they would often strip him naked, drag him into a public place, and torture or physically mutilate him for all to see. This was the British "civilizing" India.

In every case in which India had economic strength and expertise, the British intervened to shut it down in order to advance British interests. Indian textiles were a world-renowned commodity at that time. The British destroyed the Indian looms and even cut off the thumbs of weavers. They then raised tariffs on Indian imports so high as to prevent their sale in Britain, and as the industry collapsed, the British turned India into a mere exporter of cheap cotton and an importer of finished British-made textiles.

The same was done to Indian shipbuilding and Indian steel, using various tactics to collapse their market. In the case of shipbuilding, the British actually forbade the use of Indian ships in any markets in Europe or the Americas, quickly eliminating the industry in India. Similarly, with the steel industry, the British gained as much knowledge of Indian metallurgy as they could before shuttering all of India's foundries by the end of the 1700s. In both cases, Indian ships and Indian steel were widely known to be some of the best in the world. But to the British imperial mindset, the technologies and their mastery, which advance a nation as in India, are a threat to the Empire. Sir William Hicks, British Home Minister, commented in 1928: "I know it is said in missionary meetings that we conquered India to raise the level of the Indians. That is cant. We conquered India as an outlet for the goods of Britain. We conquered India by the sword, and by the sword we shall hold it. I am not such a hypocrite as to say we hold India for the Indians."

The Myth of the Railroads

One of the myths that Tharoor exposes as pure hypocrisy is that Britain's building of the Indian railroads was fundamental to India's development. On the contrary—the rail lines were built exclusively for the purpose of looting resources and crops and

Sir William Joynson-Hicks in 1923.

shipping them to ports for export. The piti-fully scant room left for actual transport of passengers was so small and overpriced that it became the subject of many political cam-paigns for the benefit of the "3rd class" Indi-ans, including by Gandhi. In a proper, human economy, large-scale capital investments, such as railroads and physical infrastructure, have a dramatic impact on the entire eco-nomic system, raising productivity and the power of the individual's labor for the entire system. In an imperial economy, however, the opposite is the case.

One reason for so much railroad investment in India was the guarantee given to investors by the British government of a minimum five per-cent annual profit—higher than any other safe investment—which was to come out of inter-nal Indian revenues when it fell short (which it always did). In addition, railroad construction was a major outlet for expensive British steel, as almost every part, from tracks to locomotives to cars, came from England. The British supplied the equipment, controlled the technology, and collected the profits, while the Indians bore the expenses and paid for the losses. While American rail-road construction cost the equivalent of £2,000/mile at that time, British rail in India cost £18,000/mile, reports Tharoor.

To make it even clearer, Tharoor includes a very tell-ing story of what the British do when mere "free trade" fails to result in the desired effect. In 1862, two repair fa-cilities were opened in India so as to begin to maintain the locomotives at home. By 1878, the Indian rail me-chanics had become so skilled at their jobs, that they began designing and manufacturing their own locomo-tives, just as good, and much cheaper than the British

The British-created Great Famine of 1943, Bengal, India.

Winston Churchill poses in the Canadian Parliament, Ottawa, Canada, December, 1941.

ones. This wouldn't stand. The British passed a law es-sentially forbidding any loco-motives from being manufac-tured in India, thereby shutting down the facilities immediately.

British Created Famines: The More Sinister Element

Winston Churchill, an outspoken but not at all unique figure in British Impe-rial history, provides a good case in point. In the great Bengal Famine of 1943, when millions were dying of star-vation, Churchill deliberately diverted food from India to already-full stockpiles for armies in Europe. When questioned about the need for relief for the Indians, Churchill merely replied that they had brought it upon themselves by "breeding like rabbits," and then asked, "Why isn't Gandhi dead yet?" On another occasion, Churchill made the spectacular comment: "I hate Indi-ans. They are a beastly people with a beastly religion."

Four million people died of starvation in Bengal in 1943.

The Bengal Famine, however, was only one among many famines in the history of the British Raj and is far from the worst. This story of the British-caused famines has already been covered by this publication[1] and does not need to be repeated here. Tharoor puts the number of Indians murdered in famines at 35 million, which, while monstrous, is itself an understatement.[2] While he does bring up Thomas Malthus in an earlier part of the book as a major influence on British policy, he doesn't develop the full significance of that influence. Malthus argued that the universal laws of nature demand that human population must only increase as much as the always limited agricultural resources will permit. Any excess will be dealt with "naturally," i.e., by death and starvation. According to this logic, the tens of millions of Indians who perished by starvation at the hands of the engorging British Empire was nothing more than this "natural" balance asserting itself. But, as Churchill himself enunciated, this was merely a justification for a policy of engineered and intentional genocide.[3] This is true British "free trade," practiced up to and including today.

The Way Out

There is much more that could be said regarding Tharoor's reports on the horrors of British rule in India, but for our purposes here, it will be sufficient to leave readers to study his book for themselves. A few other pieces of the story of the British crimes in India, elaborated by Tharoor, need to be added briefly. Education policy was shaped to foster simple manual labor and suppress intellectual and creative thought. Millions of Indians around the world were forced into indentured

Refugee trains bringing Muslims from India to Pakistan, and Hindus from Pakistan to India during Partition in 1947.

servitude by the same networks that ran the African slave trade. The previously somewhat loose caste system was transformed under the British Raj into one of rigidly bound societal status. Very important for understanding our world today, is Tharoor's presentation—though significantly understated—of the British Empire's deliberate division of Hindus and Muslims, as well as other groups in India to create what became the India-Pakistan partition of 1945-47.

As a whole, what emerges from Tharoor's book, despite his downplaying of several elements, is the pure, Zeus-like evil which characterized British rule in India, from the economic destruction, to the manipulation of minds and cultures, to the outright genocide of the multiple famines and "riot suppressions." In short, one gets a strong impression of the murderous nature of the British Empire.

This brings us to an important point. When discussing the underlying principle of different societies throughout history, Lyndon LaRouche has insisted that one must determine the *intention* of the nation or society in question. Take the case of our United States, as an example. Our historic Constitutional intention is to defend and promote in every way possible the general welfare and the public good of the nation and its citizens. Now ask yourself: What was the intention of the British in India? What could be said of the unifying idea

---

1. http://www.larouchepub.com/eiw/public/2015/eirv42n27-20150703/20-25_4227.pdf

2. *EIR* has estimated that the number was closer to 60 million, comparable to the total deaths during World War II.

3. It should not be a surprise to the witting that both the argument that human population must conform to the natural balance of nature, and the argument that human economy must conform to the natural balance of the "free market," originated in merry old England.

which characterized that history?

It is precisely here that Tharoor's book is weakest. Rather than identifying the underlying principle of empire as it manifested itself in India, he allows his story to dissolve into a sea of "complicated" factors such as wrong ideologies, greedy or racist officials, and unceasing lust for profit. While these are all true in a certain respect, this misreading of the most crucial issue diverts the reader into matters of secondary importance and fails to grasp that *it is the intention of an oligarchical empire to be criminal*—that it is a hatred of mankind that drives the oligarchical mindset.[4]

Tharoor is thorough in cataloging genocidal British atrocities. Yet, the book's weakness lies in not fully comprehending the motives behind those atrocities; it fails to perceive that, behind the surface pomp and brutality of the British colonial system, the British Empire has always been—and continues to be—axiomatically, a financial empire, an empire based on usury, debt slavery, currency manipulation and the unchallenged hegemony of the City of London. This is what we still see today in the imperial role of the IMF and WTO, and in the role of British "off-shore" financial institutions.

Tharoor's inability or unwillingness to delve deeper into the nature of the British Empire leads him into too great an emphasis on certain individual personalities, and into errors concerning key British actions. Thus, Tharoor is soft on the role of Mountbatten and Churchill. He also significantly understates Britain's overriding role in forcing through the separation of Pakistan from India at the end of British rule.

More importantly, this blindness also leads him to miss what was actually the transition from the pre-1939 British Empire into Britain's more sophisticated version of empire—which insinuated itself in the core of the financial, political, and cultural structures of the world for decades to come. After World War II, the British didn't give up their colonies because they were bankrupt and realized that the good ol' days were over, but rather decided to adapt to what was a changing postwar world. This is the history of the creation of the financial empire which exists today. This is today's trans-Atlantic financial system, and its global petrodollar, which has looted and indebted nations the world over, and which currently stands ready to disintegrate at any moment.[5]

This is the history which Lyndon LaRouche and his movement have uniquely elaborated and posed the solution for, and which must urgently be understood by any American or all people who wish to act against this evil that rules much of the world today. The time has come to destroy the British Empire for good, and in its place, establish a community of sovereign nations each committed to the common aims of mankind. To this end, let us bring the U.S., Russia, China, and India together, and bring them to the table for an agreement of this caliber, and raise the banner of creative human development for all.

---

4. Contrast this to Friedrich Schiller's essay comparing Lycurgus' Sparta with Solon's Athens, or Henry C. Carey's comparison of the American System with the British System in his *The Harmony of Interests*.

5. A recent British documentary, *The Spider's Web: Britain's Second Empire*, elaborates on the international system of tax havens which is at the core of today's Anglo-Dutch trans-Atlantic system, whose money laundering, drug trafficking, and terrorist financing play a major role in the modern-day British Empire.

Stop Club of Rome Genocide in Africa!

by Lyndon H. LaRouche, Jr.

with a new preface by Helga Zepp-LaRouche

is now available in flowing text ebook and paperback editions from Amazon.com and Google Play Books.

Today, the ideas presented in this book are rapidly being adopted and implemented around the world by more and more governments and institutions. Most importantly, the concepts in this book actually work! Poverty *can* be eliminated from the list of problems facing mankind.

This and dozens of other important EIR books are now available from Amazon.com and Google Play Books.

The FOCAC Summit
A Turning Point in Human History

This section includes five articles reporting on, and related to the just concluded Forum on China-Africa Cooperation (FOCAC) summit, which took place in Beijing, China on Sept. 3-4. This conference, attended by leaders of 53 out of 54 African nations, was a watershed event, the type of inflection point around which the entire future of the human race might turn. The message from the conference is one of hope and promise for a better future, both for Africa and for every human being throughout the world.

Africa Joins the Belt and Road

by William Jones

Sept. 5—No doubt, to the great chagrin of the representatives of the British empire and their minions in the mass media, a grand contingent of African leaders gathered in Beijing on September 3-4 for the summit of the Forum on China-Africa Cooperation (FOCAC). There the African nations made a commitment to become a "full and integral" part of China's Belt and Road Initiative. Representatives from 53 African nations—including forty heads of state, ten heads of government, and one deputy head of government—were in attendance, as well as 27 representatives of international organizations, including the Chairman of the African Union, Paul Kagame, and the Secretary General of the United Nations, Antonio Guterres. There were also 240 ministerial-level representatives among the 3,000 people in attendance at the summit.

More importantly, the growing synergy between the development plans of China and Africa has also created an important nexus of political influence for the nations of the developing world, who will now have a greater say in determining the course of history. President Xi

Xinhua/Pang Xinglei

Chinese President Xi Jinping and African leaders on their way to the opening ceremony of the Forum on Africa-China Cooperation summit, at the Great Hall of the People, Beijing, China, Sept. 3, 2018.

focused on this important element in his keynote on Sept. 3:

> To respond to the call of the times, China will get actively involved in global governance and stay committed to the vision of consultation, cooperation, and benefit for all in global governance.

China has all along played its part in promoting world peace and development, and upholding the international order. We call for increasing the representation and voice of developing countries in international affairs and [we] support efforts to strengthen the South, a weak link in the global governance system, as well as efforts to create synergy in South-South cooperation. We will continue the efforts to make the global governance system better represent the will and interests of the majority of countries, especially developing countries.

Central Role of the Belt and Road

Central to this collaboration is the Belt and Road Initiative, which serves today as the premier model for development for a world still plagued by poverty and financial crises. The whole-hearted commitment of the African countries to this program serves to promote the development of the continent, which has been so long neglected by the Western nations. Speaking as the Chairman of the African Union, President Paul Kagame of Rwanda, expressed the will of Africa very clearly: "Africa wishes to be a full and integral part of the Belt and Road Initiative." And in spite of the myriad attacks in the Western media regarding the Belt and Road's alleged "debt trap"—and its description of China's extensive involvement in Africa as a "new colonialism"—this "fake news" has not blurred the vision of Africa's leaders, who have stayed focused on the future of the continent.

These "debt trap" accusations were categorically re-

Xinhua/Ju Peng

South African President Cyril Ramaphosa, Co-Chair of the FOCAC summit, Sept. 4, 2018.

Xinhua/Li Xueren

Rwandan President Paul Kagame attends the FOCAC round table, Sept. 4, 2018.

futed at the very beginning of the summit by South Africa's President, Cyril Ramaphosa, the African co-chair of FOCAC, in his opening speech:

In the values that it promotes, in the manner that it operates, and in the impact that it has on African countries, FOCAC refutes the view that a new colonialism is taking hold in Africa, as our detractors would have us believe. It is premised on the African Union's Agenda 2063, a vision that has been crafted in Africa, by Africans. It is a vision of an integrated, prosperous, and peaceful Africa, driven by its own citizens and representing a dynamic force in the international arena.

Ramaphosa also praised the work of China's Belt and Road Initiative: "Why do we support the Belt and Road Initiative?"

Because we are confident that this initiative, which effectively complements the work of FOCAC, will reduce the costs and increase the volume of trade between Africa and China. It will encourage the development of Africa's infrastructure, a critical requirement for meaningful regional and continental integration.

China's Relationship with Africa

While the relationship of the People's Republic of China with Africa goes back 50 years to the visit of Zhou Enlai to Tanzania in 1955, it was only in 2000 that China established the Forum on China-Africa Cooperation (FOCAC) at a founding summit in Beijing. China had by then come a long way on its own path to modernization, and was beginning to play a major role as an engine for global growth. It was China's wish to share its development with the other developing countries. China's commitment to the "Third World"—as it used to be called—was always heartfelt and strong.

China also has refused to use its aid as a means of compelling these nations to change their political systems. Each of these countries has a different history and a somewhat different political structure. In contrast to the Anglo-Dutch imperial system, which has always placed political and economic "conditionalities" on its aid, China allows each country to develop in its own way and at its own pace. This was underlined by President Xi in outlining the five "No's" of China's foreign policy towards Africa, namely: "No interference in African countries' pursuit of development paths that fit their national conditions; no interference in African countries' internal affairs; no imposition of China's will on African countries; no attachment of political strings to assistance to Africa; and no seeking of selfish political gains in investment and financing cooperation with Africa."

At this point, China has become a major factor in Africa's development, having initiated more than 3,000 critical infrastructure projects on the continent, in the form of railroads, roads, dams, ports, and airports. Between 2000 and 2014, China and China-connected institutions have issued $86 billion in commercial loans. At the moment there are over 10,000 Chinese firms which have invested in Africa, or are working on Chinese-funded projects, creating over 900,000 jobs for Africans.

Upgrading the China-Africa Relationship

At the Johannesburg FOCAC summit in 2015, President Xi had introduced ten cooperation plans for Africa and committed $60 billion to implement them. Those ten plans were for industrialization, modernization of agriculture, infrastructure, financial services, green development, trade and investment facilitation, poverty reduction, public health, people-to-people exchanges, and peace and security. President Xi announced at the

Chinese Premier Zhou Enlai visiting Tanzania, June, 1965.

Beijing summit that the promised $60 billion had all been distributed to a variety of important projects. In the same speech, Xi announced that China is now prepared to upgrade the strategic partnership with the African countries, further integrating the Belt and Road Initiative with the African Union's Agenda 2063 development roadmap.

In his keynote address, President Xi said,

> To build an even closer China-Africa community with a shared future in the new era, China will, on the basis of the ten cooperation plans already adopted, launch eight major initiatives in close collaboration with African countries in the next three years and beyond.

Among the eight is an industrial promotion initiative. China will open a China-Africa economic and trade expo to promote investment in Africa. This initiative is geared to helping transform Africa from a predominantly raw materials exporter, into a producer of manufactured goods. While agriculture still weighs heaviest in African production, much effort will be put into modernizing it. Said Xi:

> We will support Africa in achieving general food security by 2030, [and] work with Africa to formulate and implement a program of action to promote China-Africa cooperation on agricultural modernization.... We will implement 50 agricultural assistance programs, provide RMB 1 billion [$150 million] of emergency humanitarian food assistance to African countries affected by natural disasters, send 500 senior agriculture experts to Africa, and train young researchers in agri-science and entrepreneurs in agri-business.

Secondly, China will promote an infrastructure connectivity program for the continent as a whole, worked out in conjunction with the African Union Agenda 2063 program. Thirdly, China will launch a trade facilitation initiative, promoting the import of manufactured products from Africa. Fourthly, China will launch a green development initiative, which will include programs for pollution prevention, desertification prevention and control, and wildlife protection. Fifthly, China will set up a capacity building initiative, which will include vocational training for young Africans. It will include the opening of an innovation cooperation center, focusing on youth and training 1,000 qualified young people for entrepreneurship in innovative industries. China is also committed to inviting 2,000 young Africans to China and will establish 50,000 government scholarships for training in Africa.

Furthermore, China will continue to move forward in the area of health care, upgrading 50 medical and health aid programs, Chinese health programs having already treated 460,000 patients in Africa. Most importantly, China will continue its peace and security initiatives, providing military aid to the African Union and supporting countries in the Sahel region, and those bordering the Gulf of Aden and the Gulf of Guinea, to uphold security and combat terrorism in those regions. China has already set up a Peace and Security Fund and a Peace and Security Forum with Africa for this purpose and is involved in combat roles in UN peace-keeping operations in Mali and South Sudan, and in non-combat medical and engineering roles in many other UN Peacekeeping operations in Africa.

Debt for Development Is No 'Trap'

In order to realize these programs, Xi said, China is prepared to commit a further $60 billion in the next three years, which would be divided up into the following categories: $15 billion of interest-free and concessional loans, $20 billion of credit lines, a $10 billion special fund for development financing, a $5 billion special fund for financing imports from Africa, and encouraging investment by Chinese firms to a level of another $10 billion.

While this again will raise hackles from the Western media over China's alleged "debt trap," China is quite prepared to meet this hoax head-on, as occurred on Sept. 4 at a press briefing with Xu Jinghu, the Special Representative of the Chinese government for African Affairs. Typically, Reuters News Agency, that long-time mouthpiece of British Imperial pretensions, posed the "debt" question.

Xu calmly went through the eight new initiatives and pointed out the beneficial effects these would have for the African people. She noted that Africa is in "the ascending phase" of its development and "faces a gap in the funding for all of these endeavors." "Africa needs capital development, and the African economy and the Chinese economy, which is more developed, are therefore complementary," she explained. Then she went into the real causes of the "debt trap" Africa may face, "You have to take into consideration the international situation. The costs of financing for development on the international market have become very expensive and most of the African countries are still dependent on exporting their raw materials. And the price of these has fallen. *That* has increased the debt of African countries a great deal."

She encouraged her Reuters interlocutor to "look closely at the African countries with the greatest debt burden and you will see that their debt is not with China." "Chinese help," Xu underlined, "is aimed at advancing Africa's development, not its debt accumulation."

Speaking at the concluding press conference, both President Xi and his African co-chair made clear that this all-important summit marked an historic watershed toward a community of shared future for mankind. Xi said:

> Together we will better uphold the common interests of China and Africa, boost the strength of developing countries, and make the world a more balanced and better place for everyone to live in. The forum was established 18 years ago. The successful hosting of the Beijing summit has brought China-Africa comprehensive strategic and cooperative partnership to a new historic starting point, and on a new journey.

In addition to the two days of intense discussion, President Xi met separately with all the government leaders who had attended, shoring up personal ties with those individuals who will be instrumental in making the FOCAC vision a reality. More than 150 joint agreements were signed in the course of the summit, including those on the joint construction of the Belt and Road. The summit issued two documents, the "Beijing Declaration—Toward an Even Stronger China-Africa Community with a Shared Future," and an Action Plan for the next three years.

Changes Underway in Africa As FOCAC Convenes

by Dean Andromidas

Sept. 8—The heads of state and other leaders of 53 African countries participated in the summit of the Forum on China-Africa Cooperation (FOCAC), an unprecedented turnout that demonstrates how the Belt and Road Initiative (BRI) is transforming relations between Africa and China. The latter committed to invest another $60 billion of concessionary funding in African infrastructural, industrial, and agricultural projects, in its win-win approach to economic and political relations. What do these words mean for the countries of Africa? Are they seen by African leaders as merely nice promises? A look at statements and economic agreements, and a sampling of representative cases from among participating nations at the summit demonstrates that the opposite is the case, that Africa is, indeed, welcoming China's expanding role in the development of Africa.

The *Chronicle* of Zimbabwe published an editorial at the close of the summit titled, "Sino-Africa Relations to Scale New Heights after FOCAC." After documenting the falseness of the claim that China is forcing Africa into a debt trap, the editorial states,

> However, contrary to this assertion, China's assistance to Africa is actually yielding tangible results, and instead of trapping African economies in debt, China-Africa co-operation under the framework of China's Belt and Road Initiative is intended to target the continent's major development bottlenecks so as to realize tangible benefits for both peoples.... On a continent where more than 600 million people still have no access to electricity, 40% of the Chinese loans go for power generation and transmission. An-

other 30% seek to modernize Africa's transport infrastructure....

It is rather ironic that Western countries are cautioning Africa against Chinese "neo-colonialism" when their own colonial past impoverished the continent by literally sucking it dry of its natural resources.

Speaking at the summit, President Emmerson Mnangagwa of Zimbabwe declared:

> Today the Road and Belt Initiative has taken everybody on board so that our economies can talk to each other, so that our economies can help each other modernize and mechanize. We are getting connected and benefiting from each other.

Enumerating the issues discussed at the summit, Mnangagwa continued:

> The issue of transportation, the issue of infrastructure development in our countries ... we believe that with this relationship under FOCAC where the rest of Africa is making conversations with China, and China [is] helping Zimbabwe and Africa to go up. And when that happens, it creates the integration of marketing in China and Africa, so we are happy that we are part of this global vision.

Mnangagwa added that China is helping Zimbabwe—

to become a middle-income country. As a result of that helping hand we leapfrog and go into a modern economy. Left alone it will take us more

A Great Change Comes for Africa   29

years to develop with our domestic investment, but given the technology, given the assistance, the financial know-how, we leapfrog and become an important cog in the global economy.

It can be said that this sentiment is near universal among the African nations now participating in the BRI. Indeed the president of the African Development Bank (AfDB), Dr. Akinwumi Adesina, told Xinhua on the sidelines of the summit, "Let me be very clear that Africa has absolutely no debt crisis; African countries are desperate for infrastructure. The population is rising, urbanization is there, and fiscal space is very small." The AfDB president added, "They are taking on a lot more debt, but in the right way."

Credits for Development

The Chinese are not heaping debts on African countries, but credits for development. A debt trap is what the European Union and the International Monetary Fund has forced on Greece, where they loaded a country of some 10 million people with over 340 billion euros of new debt, increasing its debt to Gross Domestic Product ratio from 100% to 185%. The entire sum went to German, French, British and other European banks, who themselves were more bankrupt than Greece! The austerity forced on Greece has crushed the economy, reducing economic output by one third, increasing unemployment to over 30%, and putting the country under surveillance of its

Xinhua/Yan Yan

Chinese President Xi Jinping (right) welcomes Zimbabwean President Emmerson Mnangagwa to the FOCAC Summit, Sept. 3, 2018.

Xinhua/Li Xin

Akinwumi Adesina, President of the African Development Bank.

Xinhua/Zhang Baoping

The light rail train arriving at the airport in Abuja, Nigeria, the first of its kind in West Africa, July 12, 2018.

creditors until 2060. Even the IMF, which was party to this travesty, admits the debt is unsustainable. That is a debt trap.

By contrast almost 100% of Chinese loans have gone to financing real productive investment. Statements made by African leaders at the summit reveal where the $60 billion in new investments is going. A few examples:

• Nigerian President Muhammadu Buhari told TVCNews that the loans have gone to fund infrastructure projects that "are perfectly in line with Nigeria's Economic Recovery and Growth Plan. Some of the debts, it must be noted, are self-liquidating. Nigeria is fully able to repay all the loans as and when due, in keeping with our policy of fiscal prudence and sound housekeeping."

Over the last three years, projects valued at $5 billion have been initiated, including $500 million for West Africa's first urban rail system in the Nigerian capital of Abuja, as well as a 180 km rail line connecting Abuja to Kaduna further north. Buhari said Nigeria is requesting Chinese funding to complete $3.4 billion worth of additional projects, including upgrading of airport terminals, the Lagos-Kano rail line, the Zungeru hydroelectric power project, fiber cables for Internet infrastructure, and rolling stock for the newly constructed rail lines, as well as road rehabilitation and water supply projects.

On the sidelines of the summit, the China National Petroleum Corporation (CNPC) assured the Nigerian National Petroleum

Corporation (NNPC) that it is committed to securing up to 85% of $2.8 billion to build the Ajaokuta-Kaduna-Kano (AKK) pipeline project. The pipeline will enable connectivity between the East, West and North of the country that is currently non-existent.

• On the sidelines of the summit, Egyptian President Abdel Fattah el-Sisi attended the signing of a number of agreements and contracts with Chinese companies to implement projects worth $18.3 billion, including a $4.4 billion agreement with a Chinese consortium, comprising Dongfang Electric manufacturing company and Shanghai Electric, with the Egyptian Ministry of Electricity and Renewable Energy, to build a clean coal power generation station, to be completed in six years. Also included is the construction of a petrochemical refinery plant in the Suez Canal Zone, a 2,400 MW pumped storage plant on Ataqa Mountain, the construction of the Shaodong Roi textile complex, and a Tai Chan plant for gypsum panels.

Xinhua/Li Xueren

Egyptian President Abdel-Fattah el-Sisi at the FOCAC round table, Sept. 4, 2018.

Also, the Egyptian state-owned Banque Misr announced the signing on Sept. 5 by the China Development Bank and 15 African financial institutions, of a deal to establish a Chinese-African consortium of banks.

• President Uhuru Kenyatta of Kenya secured an economic and investment cooperation agreement worth $45 million for the implementation of projects involving both nations. Also in discussion was Kenya's request for financial support for the third phase of the Standard Gauge Railway. China completed the first phase of the railway between the port of Mombasa and Nairobi, which has already revolutionized the country's transportation, dramatically reducing travel time between the two cities and increasing the throughput of the port of Mombasa by 500%. Kenya is seeking half of the $3.8 billion cost for extending the railway up to the port of Kisumu on Lake Victoria.

Pointing to the strategic importance of the extension, Kenyatta said it would open up the economic potential of other countries like Malawi, Zambia, Tanzania, Burundi, Democratic Republic of Congo, Rwanda and Uganda, as well South Sudan and Sudan, and contribute to creating a land bridge between the Indian and Atlantic Oceans.

• The President of Namibia, Hage Geingob, in his capacity as chairman of the Southern African Development Community (SADC)—the intergovernmental organization representing 16 southern African countries—appealed to China and its investment community to support the SADC region in developing its manufacturing, infrastructure, transportation, agriculture and tourism sectors.

• Gambia's attendance marked its officially becoming a member of FOCAC. President Adama Barrow has said that Gambia's membership will help the country attain the goals and objectives of the National Development Plan (2018-2021). Speaking at the Round Table Meeting on the second day of the summit, the President expressed appreciation to President Xi and the People's Republic of China for the initiative to strengthen the cooperation between China and Africa for a shared community of mutual respect and benefit.

• Zambian President Edgar Lungu and a team of ministers negotiated trade and economic agreements, including a grant of $30 million for the Lusaka East Multi-Facility Economic Zone and another $30 million interest-free loan for the reconstruction of the Mulungushi Conference Centre, in readiness for the African Union Heads of State summit in 2022. In addition, China agreed to aid the preparation of feasibility studies for the implementation of the Lusaka Mass Transit Railway Corridor project. All of these projects will contribute to the completion of the country's Seventh National Development Plan.[1]

Xinhua/Li Xueren

Kenyan President Uhuru Kenyatta at the FOCAC round table, Sept. 4, 2018.

----

1. For an in-depth study of the role of the Belt and Road Initiative in the development of Africa, please see the Schiller Institute's November 2017 study, *Extending the New Silk Road to West Asia and Africa.*

Promoting Regional Peace and Development

The momentum created by the Belt and Road Initiative in Africa has awakened a sense of optimism throughout the continent. Entire regions that have witnessed decades of both internal strife and conflicts between nations are now making peace, realizing that through a win-win approach they can participate in the great opportunities offered by the BRI. The latest example is the Horn of Africa, which just a few months ago was a region suffering from war, terrorism, and piracy. The nations there, including Ethiopia, Somalia, Djibouti, Eritrea, and South Sudan, have now embarked on the path of peace and prosperity fostered by the benevolence of the BRI.

The individual most responsible for this transformation has been Ethiopian Prime Minister Abiy Ahmed Ali, who normalized relations with Eritrea earlier this year, after almost two decades of undeclared warfare. Chinese Premier Li Keqiang held talks with Abiy in Beijing on Sept. 3, where he stated that Ethiopia is an important partner of China in Africa, and took note of the China-Ethiopia comprehensive strategic and cooperative partnership. Li also said China and Ethiopia will expand human resources development and cooperation, and promote construction of transportation infrastructure and supporting projects. China has just completed the already famous Djibouti-Addis Ababa electric railway, the landlocked country's first modern railway.

In his address to the FOCAC summit, President Mohamed Abdullahi Mohamed Farmaajo of Somalia gave fulsome praise to the role China is playing in the development of Africa through the BRI. He noted that China's lifting of 700 million people out of poverty—

holds lessons for Somalia. Somalia's coastline has historically been key to facilitating trade between China, Africa, and the Arabian Peninsula. Now, with the implementation of the Belt and Road Initiative, and our reserves of untapped resources, Somalia has the potential of becoming a driving force for regional connectivity and prosperity. By seizing these potential economic opportunities, Somalia can contribute to regional and global stability and prosperity, through win-win cooperation.

While Eritrea was not represented by its President, a high-level delegation did attend the summit. Djibouti's President, Ismail Guelleh, also attended the summit and met separately with the Chinese President. Only last July, the two countries celebrated the opening of Djibouti's new International Free Trade Zone, built with a Chinese investment of $370 million.

South Sudan's President, Salva Kiir, attended the summit. Only a few weeks ago he entered into a reconciliation process with the opposition groups that have been carrying out an armed struggle against the government. In his meeting with the Chinese President, the latter offered China's full support to the reconciliation process which, if successful, will allow the integration of the country with other regional economies.

The day after returning from Beijing, Ethiopian Prime Minister Abiy and Somali President Farmaajo arrived in Asmara, Eritrea for a tripartite summit with Eritrean President Isaias Afwerki. Up until only several weeks ago, the three countries were not on talking terms. This is the first summit of all three leaders. The leaders signed a tripartite agreement, committing them to foster comprehensive cooperation, including building close political, economic, social, cultural, and security ties; coordination to promote regional peace and security; and the establishment of a Joint High-Level Committee to coordinate their efforts in the framework of their Joint Declaration.

They agreed to help facilitate a resolution of the border dispute between Eritrea and Djibouti. In this effort the foreign ministers of the three countries flew to Djibouti on Sept. 6 to begin talks over Eritrea-Djibouti tensions. The visit by the three foreign ministers has borne fruit. Ethiopia's Foreign Minister, Workneh Gebeyehu, said on his Facebook page, "After a long period of separation, Eritrea and Djibouti have agreed to restore ties."

Confirming an agreement, Djibouti's Foreign Minister Mahmoud Ali Youssouf said: "With the truthful willingness demonstrated by Eritrea and Djibouti to make peace, all other pending issues will find their way to resolution."

Eritrea has been close to a failed state with its major export being migrants. Now, through its renewed ties with Ethiopia and other countries, Eritrea has been put firmly on the Belt and Road. Its two ports, Assab and Massawa will soon become major ports of entry for Ethiopia, a country of 108 million people. Symbolic of the potential transformation, is the docking on Sept. 5 of an Ethiopian merchant ship for the first time in twenty years at the port of Massawa.

China TV Interviews Schiller Institute's Perimony on FOCAC's World Significance

On Sept. 4, 2018, CGTN Français *of China's Global Television Network interviewed the Schiller Institute's Sébastien Périmony in Paris on "The Future of Sino-African Relations." This is an edited translation of the interview transcript. The four-minute French language* video *of the interview includes the following description: "The*

CGTN Français

Sebastian Périmony

Beijing summit of the Forum on China-Africa Cooperation has attracted the attention of experts from all over the world. Sébastien Périmony, an expert on Africa from the Schiller Institute, said the good proceedings of the summit have a profound significance for building a community of shared destiny between China and Africa."

CGTN: Sébastien Périmony has made Africa his subject of expertise, and according to him the Beijing summit, the Sino-African cooperation forum, reaches an unprecedented importance. It will enable the world to achieve common development.

Sébastien Périmony: I would say that in the 21st Century, the new name for peace is co-development. This Sino-African cooperation forum is part of this new reality, in this new paradigm, as we say today, this new economic paradigm. In Beijing, delegations representing 2.8 billion people, a third of the world's population, came together to discuss Africa's global strategic relationship with China's President Xi Jinping.... In 2015, during the FOCAC Forum on China-Africa Cooperation, Xi Jinping proposed a plan of development over three years for which China in-

vested $60 billion in the industrialization of Africa, in agricultural projects, health projects, infrastructure, and commercial services. This forum is unique in its scope: We have never seen a forum of such great importance, bringing together the largest developing country, China, and the African continent, which has the largest number of developing countries.

CGTN: President Xi Jinping, in his opening speech, spoke of China's continued respect for Africa, the country's love and support for the continent, and Beijing's adherence to the principle of "five no's." This is an important aspect for Mr. Périmony, who also said that sincere friendship and equality of treatment have become a reality, where common development is achieved through the efforts made, and not by imposing one's will on others.

Périmony: It's a new system, an inclusive system. We do not interfere in the affairs of others, we work on common projects to improve the living standard of citizens.

CGTN: In his speech, President Xi Jinping mentioned the six pillars on which construction is built, a community of common destiny. Mr. Périmony believes that the Beijing summit will not only open up new prospects for development, but also promote the tripartite co-

CGTN Français

Manufacturing facility in Africa.

operation among France, China, and Africa, and high-light their respective advantages by moving hand in hand.

Périmony: The dynamic development of infra-structure, agricultural modernization, professional training, and health care will continue to develop. It is a paradigm that is unstoppable today. Africa will develop. It's going to be up to France to realize that this change is underway and participate in this change. I think that China and France must develop a joint project in Africa and make that a symbol of tripartite cooperation among France, Africa, and China.

CGTN: Westerners describe China's African policy as neocolonialism, but according to Sébastien Péri-mony, these accusations are unjustified.

Périmony: Today, when we talk about neocolonial politics, and we look at Africa, no one in Africa is ac-cusing China of a neocolonial policy. We can blame the former colonialists for what they have done in Africa. Moreover, look at these countries, take the example of France. There are still 14 countries that are under finan-cial supervision, using a currency that is controlled by the French Treasury and the Eurozone called the "CFA franc." There are still 14 countries, 200 million people, who have no access to their own credit, budget, or deficits. Being polite, you would call this "monetary servitude," and less politely said, it is "economic colonialism."

CGTN: Mr. Périmony looks forward to cooperation and the future in Sino-African relations. The construc-tion of a community of common destiny between China and Africa will have a positive impact on the harmonious development of human society and common progress.

Périmony: I would say that we are witnessing a revolutionary change, a new international monetary and financial paradigm which, after 30 years of being stuck in a so-called free market economy, the world is returning to that which is essential—the development of man—education, healthcare, agriculture, and self-sufficiency. That is the new paradigm which China has initiated: It will spread throughout the world.

Berlin Lake Chad Conference: German Government Not Interested in Transaqua

by Elke Fimmen

BERLIN, Sept. 4—At a two-day, high-level conference on the Lake Chad region, Sept. 3-4 in Berlin, 70 na-tions, international organizations, and civil society actors met to discuss humanitarian help, stabilization, and development cooperation for the Lake Chad region, one of the poorest areas of Africa. Organized by the German Foreign Office in cooperation with the Norwe-gian and Nigerian governments, participants in the con-ference pledged $2.17 billion in aid for the coming years, plus concessionary credits of $467 million. German Foreign Minister Heiko Maas, who opened the conference, said that Germany will contribute 100 mil-lion euros for the region by 2020 and 40 million euros for crisis prevention and stabilization, of which 30 mil-lion euros is a new commitment. In terms of develop-ment funds, Germany has contributed 220 million euros at present, with new projects in preparation. As of this writing, the projects for which the pledged sums are specifically to be used, are not known.

UN/Loey Felipe

Heiko Maas, German Minister for Foreign Affairs.

The Berlin conference, which was a follow-up to a 2017 Oslo event, heard reports from high-level repre-sentatives from Niger, Chad, Nigeria, and Cameroon, ministers and governors of the most affected regions, in addition to NGOs and international organizations such as the UNDP, World Bank, European Union, and African Union. Secretary General of the Lake Chad Basin Commission (LCBC) Mamman Nuhu, from Chad, was also a featured speaker at two sessions, addressing the strategic situation, the improved regional cooperation, and new responsibilities of the Commission, which has now become the main coordinator for regional and international contacts in the region.

In the setting of this conference, however, the real game-changer for the future of the region, namely the proposed Transaqua project, was entirely left out and was clearly not wanted. Mr. Nuhu, the authoritative person for briefing the assembled international audience about this project, could only refer to "replenishing of the lake" at the end of his speech—on the panel about crisis prevention and stabilization—and he said, unfortunately, he had no time to discuss it.

And Günter Nooke, Commissioner for Africa of the German Economic Cooperation and Development Ministry, and advisor to Chancellor Angela Merkel, quipped, seemingly out of the blue, that the water from the Congo River does not solve the problems of the region. Instead he promoted private initiatives such as setting up businesses of one to three persons. He made these remarks in the afternoon plenum session on sustainable development, moderated by UNDP Administrator Achim Steiner.

Transaqua is the proposal, strongly backed by the Schiller Institute,[1] for rebuilding and further developing the entire watershed of the region, and massively expanding desperately needed fresh water supplies. It has been identified as a model for successful African-European-Chinese cooperation, and Transaqua is precisely such a transformative project, which is coherent with the intention of the just-concluded FOCAC Summit in Beijing.

But the topic, and the reality, of the existing dynamic of win-win cooperation—with the FOCAC meeting taking place simultaneously with the Berlin conference—could not be entirely ignored, as *EIR* cor-

UNDP/Lamine Bal

Representatives of donors and multilateral financial institutions at Lake Chad Conference, Berlin, Germany, Sept. 3, 2018.

respondents brought up Transaqua, both in the morning session of NGOs before the official opening, and in a special, afternoon briefing with Achim Steiner, one of the main organizers of the conference. Here is the transcript of *EIR*'s Stephan Ossenkopp's question to Steiner, and Steiner's answer during that briefing.

Ossenkopp: My colleague attended the Abuja Lake Chad conference in February of this year and was very enthusiastic, because they have adopted the Charter of Abuja, a roadmap, where they acknowledged that the entire crisis can only be solved by a major infrastructure intervention.

Eight heads of state, including the LCBC, put Transaqua into the roadmap, bringing water from the Congo to the Chad Basin. There is a joint venture already being set up by the Italian and Chinese governments for financing a feasibility study. This project can be built within 10-15 years. PowerChina is looking into the possibility of building it within 12 years.

I am wondering why this is not addressed at a high-level conference such as this? This could bring hope to the people, because humanitarian aid is always short-term and crisis-oriented. But a development perspective could mean a game-changer.

Steiner: Very briefly, all ideas are welcome, all partners are welcome. And this conference that we co-convened with Germany, Norway, and Nigeria, has its origins in a crisis which required a humanitarian response and has now become part of how in a broader

---

1. See https://schillerinstitute.com/extending-new-silk-road-west-asia-africa/

way we can build out from that response to that crisis, to longer-term development. It is not—and that is why the Abuja conference happened as a free-standing conference—the only place where future development decisions are discussed. In that sense, I am aware of this project.

As you can imagine, the financial implications of this project [Transaqua] exceeds by the factor X the financial volumes we are talking about here. For us it's not in the immediate realm of relevance, because it simply cannot be financed through the tracks that we can mobilize right now. But we also attended parts of the discussion. Whether you start with the basin transfers or whether you start with the restoration of Lake Chad, I think we will find that sometimes these very heavy infrastructure interbasin transfer schemes may in the long term prove financially viable or they may not prove viable. Damming the Congo River in order to produce power for the whole of Africa has existed as a project for the last 30 years. It's simply… there are other factors that play a role.

But what I want to end with is to say: Look, there are already a number of other measures being taken to address the ecological restoration of Lake Chad. So you don't have to spend billions to try to bring this lake back to life. You have examples like the Lake Faguibine in Mali, which had to be abandoned because of the civil strife. Lake Chad is today one-twentieth of what its size was in 1963.

This is significantly the consequence of developmental decisions that have been taken that can in part be reversed and that can be also compensated for with measures to restore at least parts of that lake. Wherein it is then financially, economically, and ecologically rational to invest in an interbasin transfer, is something that I am sure Transaqua will continue to promote as an option. And I think we will see whether the economics of it makes it attractive enough.

So the simplest way to say it, is: We have a whole range, a spectrum of interventions. We are at one end, the humanitarian plus development and stabilization. On the other end are mega-infrastructure interventions that may materialize in 5, 10 or 20 years.

That was Steiner's response.

The official representative of the Embassy of China in Berlin had also spoken in the plenary session about the FOCAC meeting as an example of China's commitment to help alleviate the problems of the region, and of its willingness to collaborate with all international actors to this effect.

German Business Wants To Work with China in Africa

The following is an edited translation, from the original German, of an interview with Stefan Liebing, Chairman of the Afrika-Verein der deutschen Wirtschaft (Africa Association of German Business), which was conducted July 5, 2018, on the sidelines of the German-African Business Day, organized by the Afrika-Verein in Berlin. The interview was conducted by EIR's Stephan Ossenkopp.

Stephan Ossenkopp: In your introductory speech [at the German-African Business Day] you mentioned the BRICS countries, as possible competitors in Africa. How are German or European relations proceding with the BRICS countries vis-a-vis Africa? Are there any possibilities for cooperation?

conjuncta.com
Stefan Liebing

Stefan Liebing: There are a lot of things that we can learn from the Chinese. There are also things we should not learn. As far as standards are concerned, and perhaps quality, I believe that Germany is already more in the lead. But there are a number of things we can learn from the Chinese, and one of them is establishing closer links with African governments. In Africa, economic decisions are always politically driven, there are very close links

Voith, a German engineering company, provided turbines such as this one for joint projects with China.

between government and the private sector. I believe that we are not so good at this—not only in insuring private investments, securing them, and issuing guarantees, but also, for example, in speaking with one voice, and presenting concepts and package deals as "Germany, Inc."

Many of my African friends tell me that they would like to work with the Germans, and not only with the Chinese, but they often have no choice. If African nations advertise for bids—"Who can build us a large infrastructure corridor with road, pipeline, refinery, and port?"— they find no one in Germany who can do it all. What the Chinese government does is—they turn around and say: "Here's the Ex-Im Bank for financing; here's the construction company; here are oil and gas companies—we can pull this together." There are structural things we can learn here.

Tackle Some Things Together with China

In addition, I believe that we have things that we can tackle together, too. Above all, I see infrastructure projects that always have a large building component, and then a high-tech component. Look at Voith [a large German mechanical engineering firm], it has established cooperation with the Chinese such that the high technology components and turbines come from Germany, and the construction capability to build a big dam—which is often 70-80% of the order for a hydroelectric power plant—is what the Chinese construction companies are providing. Incidentally, in Germany we hardly have construction companies active in Africa any more. So that's why it makes a lot of sense to join forces where you have strengths that complement each other, rather than compete directly.

Ossenkopp: A report by the Federal Ministry of Economics makes it fairly clear that we have lost the ability to deliver turnkey projects. Is that not a big loss, and shouldn't we actually be able to restore those skills?

Liebing: Yes, of course it's a loss, but one must say that plant engineering is something that is technologically, in many cases, no longer the pinnacle of established technologies. And in many areas there are things that the Chinese and Asians can do, that you can get just as well in South Korea as in Germany. That's been the course of development. At one point we were also at the top of the textile industry. We are not any longer, because we are too expensive and there is no technological edge. So there will always be industries that move from Germany to the emerging markets, because the emerging countries will eventually be able to handle these industries. Then we will often be too expensive with our standards of quality.

That is why I believe that this is not a bad thing, per se, in a world that is still hopefully driven by multilateral free trade, if we cannot deliver turnkey projects from a single source. But it will be important to reflect on how we can cooperate with companies and other countries in such a way that our high-tech components, where we continue to be leaders, are compatible with what others may offer more cheaply.

For example, nobody in the world needs Germany to screw a car together. Any Indian company can do that too. So can Russia, and the Chinese. But no other nation can build an S-Class automobile. That's why the [Mercedes-Benz] S-Class continues to be driven by all governments, because it's the best car in the world.

In other words, we need to carefully maintain our strengths and take advantage of the technological leading edge to bring it all together in one package. The VW [automobile] plant in Rwanda works in cooperation with the CFAO [an automotive distribution firm in Africa, subsidiary of Toyota], which arose from an Afri-

can-French company, as regards the concrete implementation on site. There are many such partnerships, and there is much more to be done with Asia than before.

Ossenkopp: A big China-Africa summit will take place in September. There is evidence that Africa is turning away from established industrialized countries, to China, regardless of the political model, as China has managed to lift 700 million of its people out of poverty over the past 40 years, which is also Africa's primary goal. How do you see this development?

Africa Not Turning Away from Europe

Liebing: There are several aspects. I do not see the development as Africa turning away from Europe toward China. On the contrary, I have the impression that, as far as economic cooperation is concerned, the links are weakening: China is diverting funds to the Silk Road Initiative, which only marginally affects Africa, in East Africa and the ports, but is otherwise largely ignored. My feeling is there are less soft loans, less concessional financing from China in Africa for the big infrastructure projects. At the same time, I see people turning back to Europe for both quality and political reasons. Look at the change of power in South Africa, which certainly has not led to more orientation to China but rather, under the new president, is more likely to head back toward Europe.

If you ask whether Africans are guided by the Chinese model as a blueprint for their own development, then the question is, do Africans want to implement a similar political and economic model, state-sponsored capitalism, so to speak? I would say there are some cases, yes—Ethiopia is such an example. And maybe there are things that make sense. To get things rolling with a little more economic coordination, a big push for infrastructure—I wouldn't exclude that. But in general, I don't actually see such a tendency, but the opposite.

Ossenkopp: You mentioned the Silk Road Initiative, which has changed the attitude of many countries which were previously critical of China. I'll bring up Japan, which is making relatively strong overtures to China. There was a Silk Road Summit in Beijing last year, to which Prime Minister Abe sent the chairman of his party. It is believed that Abe will visit China this year to negotiate foreign trade rules in order to work with China to develop third countries such as in Africa. Is this development relevant for Western European countries, which often have reservations about China?

Liebing: To be honest, I think we should do something similar. We should push that too. I have simply said that it makes a lot sense for Germany and similar countries to do something together with China in third countries, because there are certain areas that the Chinese can cover well, while we hardly do them any longer, or at least we can only compete with difficulty. When we get this collaboration, it's ultimately a very similar model.

I call them "trilateral approaches." Two developed countries or regions working together to bring something meaningful to Africa. Last year, we did a whole series of events to which we invited Japanese representatives and said, "What can we do, Germany and Japan, together in Africa?" We did something similar with China. I am in contact with the Chinese Ambassador and the German government, and I hear that the Chinese government also regularly makes the same proposals to the German government: Let us work together to jointly develop third markets. I believe that one has to get away from the sort of assessment which says: "Look at the wicked Chinese; they want to take Africa away from us."

Again, there are things that can be improved when it comes to standards: safety, labor, health and environmental standards, and quality standards. We can certainly contribute something to the cooperation. But we must get away from this demonization of Chinese involvement on the continent. If we do it together, it can only get better—better for the Africans, because we may also bring a different view of things as far as the form of cooperation is concerned. Therefore: [in English] *if you can't beat them, join them.* Let us tackle it together and bring our strengths.

Africa Infrastructure Funding Alternatives

Ossenkopp: The Asian Infrastructure Investment Bank (AIIB) has now developed into a comprehensive, multilateral financing organization. Even the European Council on Foreign Relations (ECFR) says it is not the counter-model to the World Bank or the counter-model against the West, as it has often been described in the press. It's a $100 billion fund, and the Contingent Reserve Arrangement (CRA) adds another $100 billion. Also, the Silk Road Fund, which is important for Africa with $55 billion, has already been visited by a Bundesbank representative. Can we use such multilateral instruments through the Federal Ministry of Finance and the Bundesbank to jointly finance projects in Africa?

Liebing: That's a start. It is really only a beginning. I myself am a big fan of this Africa50 initiative, where the Africans themselves set up such an infrastructure fund. Half of the African governments have since joined. They have already put together a billion. The "Friends of Africa50" were also here, talking to the German government. The plan is to start with three billion. If you expect that you can manage now with an equity ratio of perhaps 30%, that means you can build 10 billion worth of infrastructure.

I do not think we have a shortage of funds for infrastructure, but we have a bottleneck on bankable projects. And for that you need funds, high-risk capital, which you can put into early stages of development. Once you have a project that is ready for construction, complete with all contracts, warranties, and insurance, you will find much more money in the world than you can use. The problem is the phase from idea to construction, and financing that is what Africa50 does with its budgets.

We have suggested to the German government that it offer insurance for German companies for the project development phase. A German project developer for a wind farm in Africa, has to pay out 4-5 million euros, before he even knows whether he can invest and make

money: This is the cost of studies, securing land, lawyers, flying out there, and whatever else. We said, "Let's create an insurance model." If this investor succeeds, he will of course pay an insurance premium and reduce his profits a bit. If the investment does not succeed, he will be reimbursed part of his upfront costs from this insurance....

I am relatively sure that this will easily multiply the number of infrastructure projects that we will do with relatively little money.... With a constant probability of success, that would mean, yes, we will also double the number of projects that are built in the end, with relatively little money.

These are things we are currently trying to discuss with the German government. Of course you can do that multilaterally. Africa50 may spend and invest 10% of the funds for such early stages. To be honest, I couldn't care less how we organize it. Whether we give German development money to an Asian development bank, which then works through the Chinese with our partners in Africa—there are others who may have better ideas on how to structure it, and I have no idea how best to save on taxes or other such things.

For me, the point is, we have to do it! We have suggested how such things can be organized. But I am very open—if someone comes along who is smarter and has better suggestions, then we can do it in a different way. It just has to be done now. And we have been discussing this for a year. One year ago today we met with the president [President Alpha Condé of Guinea] on the eve of the G-20 summit. One year ago we started to discuss this with the German government. For a year none of this has been implemented, and that's what I find so annoying for the German entrepreneurs.

MAY 1, 2009

The Real 'New Bretton Woods': A Dollar-Based Global Recovery

by Lyndon H. LaRouche, Jr.

The issue to be considered here, is the presently greatest political obstacle in the pathway of rallying needed political support for adoption of a readily available economic recovery of the United States, and, thus, potentially, the planet as a whole. The impediment is the still prevalent, stubborn ignorance of the difference between, on the one side, the monetary system of a Europe dominated by imperial London, and, in the opposition, a national-credit system of the type implicit in the U.S. Federal Constitution. For the planet as a whole, a global network of what are, respectively, perfectly sovereign national credit systems of the type intended by President Franklin Roosevelt (until the change which came in April 13, 1945 under U.S. President Harry S Truman), is the only possible defense of the world's economy against this planet's presently accelerating general breakdown-crisis.

For example: This is the same problem which was typified by the blunder in a recent proposal which was mistakenly named "A New Bretton Woods." That was a scheme recently foisted upon some important Russian and Italian officials in a meeting at Modena, Italy.

The notable culprits for that occasion, included such as a certain U.S. mathematician well known to me, Dr. Jonathan Tennenbaum. Tennenbaum, who had once known better, was, morally, the worst of the several hoaxsters among the witting participants for that occasion, because of his recently assumed credentials as a turncoat. The present report which follows here, should be considered a remedy for the hoax represented by Dr. Tennenbaum's proposed measures, but, as I shall point out here, my report here is a much-needed warning against the numerous, currently circulating frauds spawned either by the "global warming" hoax of Britain's Prince Philip, or other schemes similar to Dr. Tennenbaum's own, schemes which are, each and all, opposed to those principles of a science of economy on which the avoidance a planetary plunge into a new dark age now depends, immediately.

*The following is, in its aims, essentially a scientific work; but, when we examine the causes of the physical effects of man's hand, we must turn our attention, as I do here, and as Percy Shelley did in his **A Defence of Poetry**, to that power of Classical artistic insight which reigns over the creative mind of our greatest scientists and statesmen, a power of creativity which resides, as Shelley wrote in his **A Defence of Poetry**, in the dynamic, creative, poetic potentialities of the human mind.*

FOREWORD: **The American System**
A May-Day Recollection

The most popular, and what has also been, repeatedly, the immediately most ruinous among the widely spread delusions among nations of the world today, is the delusory presumption, that the prices which are mistakenly regarded as being properly assigned to

Alexander Hamilton created the American System of political-economy, which is at the core of the U.S. Constitution. Portrait by Daniel Huntington, 1865.

commodities by markets, when considered "statistically," should converge "naturally" upon what is foolishly named "a scientific measurement of value." There is nothing actually scientific about any of that practice.

The more knowledgeable we might become in these matters, the greater the importance of today's virtual ignorance of true history. Even when what is presented as being an historical account, is not false as to facts listed, as the old schools of history have been dying out from their former place in universities, what has come to pass as a substitute for history, have been, at their least worst, as merely chronicles. The tendency has been to focus on the behaviors of particular individuals, but leave aside that most essential distinction of mankind from beasts, the role of the evolution of culture, and, thus, the reciprocal relations, spanning successive generations, even across millennia, in which the substrate of the motives of societies and their individuals has been laid down. Those cultural strata extended from ancient into modern times, are the domain which the reacting minds of the living individuals and their cultures inhabit; it is developments, such as crucial change, emerging out of that deeply-reaching background, which speak to us of new things, but as also a speaker of a voice from ancient times.

So, we act on the past, but, in the medium of human culture, the past also reacts for, or against a present development, thus speaking with voices out of the historical depths of cultures of preceding generations.

To know history, wish to go where it happened, and hear, in informed imagination, the truly spoken voices of those who lived there in past times. We can, in a certain degree, do much of that, as our available resources may permit this; but, whatever may be the case on those accounts, we must, at the very least, relive the past in our minds as if we had actually been there when it happened, such that we hear the voice of real history speaking to our mind's ears.

Proceed, therefore, as follows.

The Awful Thing Nixon Did

U.S. President Richard Nixon, did not actually cause the present world monetary-financial and economic-breakdown crisis. However, the present world crisis, whose official launching came under the administration of George W. Bush, Jr., could not have occurred as it did, without Nixon's resumption of a "free trade" system, which represented a radical turn away from the constitutional American System of political economy. In the course of this present report, among other things, the crucial, broader implications of Nixon's particular role in launching the present world crisis should begin to be clear.

The root of this, and many earlier global tragedies can be fairly pinned on the world-famous delusion of Adam Smith, a delusion adopted by such dupes of a "free trade" doctrine as Karl Marx. This delusion has been typical of the kind of forms of high-flown popular nonsense which has now finally succeeded in leading the world as a whole, over decades, into this present planetary breakdown-crisis. The essence of the mental disorder which I have exposed in the following pages, is the pathetic belief that a statistical process of events converges upon what the behaviorists see as a particular form of a relative social value which the credulous presume to be a "self-evidently natural," standard

National Archives/Richard Nixon Library

President Richard Nixon's resumption of a British free trade system in 1971 was a radical turn away from the American System of political-economy. Here, Nixon campaigning for the Presidency in 1968.

choice of natural measurement of either financial net gains, or of losses, of either national economies, or even the world economy considered as a whole. British economist Piero Sraffa's novel, 1975 **Production of Commodities by Means of Commodities,** is, speaking clinically, among the relatively more striking, if nonetheless perverse illustrations of the kind of folly which underlies such popular delusions, delusions of not only persons, but most of the leading governments of the world, so far, today.[1]

Therefore, when all relevant evidence bearing on that point is considered, to save the world from a virtual sojourn in Hell, let the world now abandon the fetish of that present global disease of monetarism associated with the memory of such assets of the British East India Company's Lord Shelburne as the utterly depraved Adam Smith and Jeremy Bentham.

Contrary to "Old Adam" Smith and Bentham, the conceptions on which actually competent views of modern European economy depend, had been introduced earlier, chiefly, by two works by the Fifteenth Century's great Cardinal Nicholas of Cusa. The first was Cusa's argument for the institution of what

became the modern sovereign nation-state republic, his A.D. 1433 **Concordancia Catholica**; the second, his foundation of modern European physical science, in his A.D. 1440 **De Docta Ignorantia.** It was France's King Louis XI who established the first modern nation-state republic consistent with Cusa's **Concordancia Catholica**, a French republic whose stunningly successful, revolutionary achievement, was soon emulated by Louis XI's admirer, England's Henry VII.

It was Cusa's **De Docta Ignorantia**, echoing, in part, the spirit of science in Filippo Brunelleschi's work, which had established a competent form of modern European science in general, and, therefore, also the principles of physical economy. It had been that Cusa who inspired Leonardo da Vinci and, also, that founder of modern physical scientific practice, Leonardo follower Johannes Kepler. That was the Kepler, who remains, as Albert Einstein emphasized, still today, not merely the uniquely original founder of a modern science of physical astronomy on which all humanity's essential scientific progress thereafter has depended, to this present time; Kepler's discoveries established the modern practice of a truly universal quality of a competently practiced physical science and its method.

Throughout the following pages, the principal theme will be, that the essence of any competent modern scientific practice, including that underlying the successful practice of national economy, lies in the recognition that the human faculties of sense-perception, such as sight and hearing, are not, in themselves, the substance of reality, but are merely a needed form of inborn instrumentation for observing some selected aspects of human sense-experience, aspects of actually sensed experiences which, taken only by themselves, are merely the shadows cast by reality, not the actual content, not the actual cause of that experience.

Actual knowledge of the real universe is not accessible through the senses as such, but only through the creative powers of the human individual mind, which is the power to adduce the efficient reality which is apprehended as the fruit of the creative powers of mind. That

---

1. **Production of Commodities by Means of Commodities: Prelude to a Critique of Economic Theory** (Cambridge: Cambridge University Press, 1975).

task can be realized only through insight into the problematic nature of the mere, shadow-like experience of the individual's sense-perceptions. Contrary to Aristotle and Newton, as also Paolo Sarpi's followers generally, it is not in the mere data of sense-perceptions that we actually know the efficient universe we inhabit; like Kepler's uniquely original general formulation for the effect of gravitation, the mathematical image is always merely the reflection of the principle which casts such shadows.

Although it was the formulation, provided by Kepler's **The Harmonies of the World**, for a general principle of Solar gravitation, which remains the only competent formulation for gravitation supplied by any source, the mathematical formula itself is not the actual principle of gravitation; rather, the mathematical formulation, which as Albert Einstein saw, science owes uniquely to Kepler, is a description of the shadow-like effect of the actual principle of gravitation. This discovery by him occurred as the next crucial step in scientific progress, following the success of Kepler in making his preceding, original, discovery of the notion of "equal areas, equal times."[2]

So, the essential, systemic fallacy within Aristotle's system, and that of his follower Euclid, is now to be located in the matter of their asserted *a-priori* notions of mere sense-certainty. So, as Philo of Alexandria rebuked the followers of Aristotle in Philo's own lifetime, as in the case of Aristotle himself, creativity does not actually occur within the confines of what mere mathematics treats as if it were the universe. Notably, Aristotle, would not have permitted even the Creator of the universe to perform a creative action within that universe, once the idea of a fixed universe were established in a fixed form of motions defined from the standpoint of sense-certainty. Thus, for Aristotle, once the crafting of the universe is presumed to have been completed, even the Creator himself could not alter that fixed scheme. Creativity as such is the great issue of science and economy.

It were as if the Olympian Zeus of Aeschylus' **Prometheus Bound** (or, perhaps, Dostoyevsky's "Grand Inquisitor") had commanded the Creator to cease creating.

That denial of a continuing role of the creative powers of the Creator, as that denial was premised systemically on the method of Aristotle, is a denial which is now customarily presented as a reductionist's notion of a "Second Law of Thermodynamics." That so-called "law," actually introduced as a mere, arbitrary mathematical formalist's presumption by Rudolf Clausius and Hermann Grassmann, which was merely imposed upon the widely taught practice of science, then, has become the present time's premise for the crucial, and actually implicitly criminal presumption deployed presently, by the followers of Britain's Prince Philip and his, and his dupes' Nazi-like, pro-genocidal hoax, the World Wildlife Fund.

These followers of Paolo Sarpi, such as that Prince Philip, are more wildly radical in this way than Aristotle. That shame is a point of pride for them, since they are the avowed true followers of the medieval irrationalist William of Ockham. It has been on that presumed authority that these modern followers of medieval Ockham permit themselves to innovate in shameless ways forbidden to the strict devotees of Aristotle's dogma; however, at their bottoms, both Aristotle and Ockham share in common their denial of the existence of knowledge of actual principles of our universe.[3] It is that wildly irrational superstition taught by those Liberals otherwise known as the empiricists, which is the essence of that evil, known as Liberalism; it has been the influence of that Liberalism itself, which has become the origin of the presently threatened onrushing doom of the world's nations and peoples today.

In the eyes of the Creator, the followers of Britain's Prince Philip today, the so-called "zero-growthers," are the real-life children of Satan amok on our planet today. It could be said of them, that, "While the faithful of Aristotle grow cobwebs in Purgatory, the followers of Britain's Prince Philip appear to have been born in a Hell of their own making, from which they have never departed, and, perhaps, never will." With that judgment of mine, I believe that true poets will agree.

---

2. The set of hoaxsters who provided Isaac Newton with a plagiarism of Kepler's formulation, did add an exact value for an important term of the formulation supplied by Kepler, but the formula credited to Newton represented a fraudulent claim by Newton's associates. Newton had actually discovered nothing. It was these two discoveries in astrophysics, by Kepler, which were the specific prompting of Gottfried Leibniz's uniquely original discovery (no later than 1676, in Paris) of the infinitesimal calculus.

3. Adam Smith, **Theory of Moral Sentiments** (1759).

EIRNS/James Rea

*The followers of Britain's Prince Philip, the "zero-growthers,"
are the real-life children of Satan today. Their anti-scientific
policies of deindustrialization will doom the majority of the
world's population.*

The Fight for Human Creativity!

Despite all that philosophical reductionism, it is actual creativity, that human creativity which does not exist among lower forms of life, which is the essential nature of the functional economic distinction of mankind from the beasts, and which is also the prerequisite of societies' continued existence as physical economies.

That point is more readily understood by a reference to the ban on human knowledge of creativity ("fire") of the Olympian Zeus of Aeschylus' **Prometheus Bound.** There is nothing merely fictional, in itself, in Aeschylus' description of Zeus's frankly Satanic motives. As in today's systemically pro-fascist, "environmentalist movement," the ban on creative innovations of physical-scientific practice by some human beings, has continued to be the universal policy of globally extended European imperialism until today, since ancient Greece submitted to the zero-scientific-growth dogma of what was known already in those times as "the oligarchical principle" which has served, ever since the time of Philip of Macedon, as the most fundamental doctrine of oligarchical law of all empires, including that of the household of Queen Elizabeth II and her depraved consort, today.

In contrast to that frankly pro-Satanic, "zero growth" characteristic of the policy of today's so-called "Greenie" accomplices such as Prince Philip and former U.S. Vice-President and present hoaxster Al Gore, all competent efforts on behalf of modern scientific progress in the practice of political economy, have been a reflection of a development of modern creative scientific thought, in both physical science generally, and along the lines of modern practice of physical economy pioneered by such as Cusa, Leonardo, Kepler, Fermat, and Leibniz. This I shall show in the text which follows this introduction.

Today, we must concede, without exception, that the world as a whole is in the present grip of a general breakdown-crisis. Today's world crisis is not naturally an inevitable one; rather, it is the fruit of increasingly insane, and also utterly immoral, but, nonetheless ruling doctrines of physical-economic stagnation gathered under the presumptions of a combined doctrine of "zero growth" and "free trade." It is most notable, that these wicked presumptions were already specific to that so-called "British Empire" which was founded, in a treaty of February 1763, upon the specific dogmas of a certain Venetian school of the founder of modern European Liberalism, Paolo Sarpi.

There we have the essential moral issue of controversy confronting all mankind immediately today:

The situation of the entire world today, is such that, unless we promptly uproot those dogmas of behaviorism in the tradition of Adam Smith and Jeremy Bentham which permeate the present British imperial "free trade" system, the entire planet will soon be plunged into a prolonged new dark age for all humanity. Therefore, we must spend a few more words in this introduction, on the matter of the errant state of mind by which, in the main, the nations of the world are still being governed, top down, today.

In contrast to those Liberal sources to which I have made reference above, silly ideas such as those of the empiricist school of Paolo Sarpi's followers, are not natural, except as we, in summing up the case just stated, might view them as a natural consequence of ideas whose lunatic premises are products of that unnatural, and intrinsically evil form of political-economy, which is known, interchangeably, as imperialism, monetarism, or, in the worst expression, the behaviorism which is taught among such duped followers of Paolo Sarpi as the Eighteenth-century devotees of the methods of Rene Descartes.

More significant on this account, is the fact that the delusion responsible for the seemingly periodic collapses of leading economies of the world, as during the course of more than two recent centuries, can be summed-up here and now as having been the natural consequence of the intrinsic incompetence of the belief in those fictions promoted by such representatives of the teachings adopted and spread during the late Seventeenth through Nineteenth centuries, as by the influence of Paolo Sarpi, and by the British East India Company's Haileybury School. These have been taught, as that belief has been expressed by John Locke, David Hume, the Physiocrats Francois Quesnay and A. R. J. Turgot, Adam Smith, and the British Foreign Office's essentially brutish Jeremy Bentham, Thomas Malthus, Immanuel Kant, and David Ricardo.

The patterns of behavior to be considered on that account, can not be fully and competently understood, until we have adopted the standpoint of *dynamics*, which has been carried into modern times from the ancient, Classical Greek notion of *dynamis*, and, which was revived to this effect, as a term of modern science, *dynamics*, during the 1690s, by Gottfried Leibniz. This notion, which was actually expressed implicitly in the development of modern science by Cardinal Nicholas of Cusa, and such among his followers as Leonardo da Vinci, Johannes Kepler, and Pierre de Fermat, was not formally developed by name, in modern science usage, until the work of Leibniz; but, it has been the leading principled feature of competent modern science and also Classical artistic composition since Leibniz's initiative.

The concept of dynamics, so situated, is also the indispensable standpoint of Classical artistic composition, such as Classical poetry and music, and Classical tragedy. It embraces, thus, the full sweep of the notion of the idea of culture, including the subject of the characteristics of the processes of the human mind. This is expressed most beautifully in the closing paragraph of Percy Bysshe Shelley's **A Defence of Poetry**; there, it represents the same kind of notion as Riemannian physics generally, and the Classical irony of history as Shelley emphasizes that in that closing paragraph. It is the same conception, in principle, which underlies the notion of a true universal physical principle, such as Kepler's uniquely original discovery of the principle of gravitation, as presented in his **The Harmonies of the World**.

War, Money & Empire

The prevalence of various forms of Liberal delusions, has not been exactly original with modern practices as such. It echoes all of the principal known European imperialist practices, that since no later than the role of the Apollo-Dionysos cult flanked by the monetarism expressed by the set of treasuries at Delphi. It is to be recognized as both the authorship of what became the Peloponnesian war, and as a presently continuing, traditionally leading monetarist power of oligarchism long operating within the Mediterranean region. This legacy of that intrinsically evil, ancient Delphi cult, has been expressed in the virtually axiomatic presumptions underlying the character of the Roman Empire, of Byzantium, and, also, of both the Habsburg and those Anglo-Dutch Liberal imperial systems which had been spawned by the monetary agency of Venice, since about A.D. 1000.[4]

Today's institution of still-reigning Anglo-Dutch Liberal imperialism, was first established as the empire of a private company, the British East India Company, by the February 1763 Peace of Paris. This British imperialism is to be understood, still today, in all its functionally essential features, as a modern continuation of that form of European-based, maritime imperialisms made in the Satanic likeness of the Roman empire, an image which has customarily ruled, even before imperial Rome, in recurring varieties of transmogrifications,

---

4. The specifically European oligarchical tradition of today is traced from the Delphic interests which had spawned the Peloponnesian War, and which were Plato's immediate adversaries in opposing his plan for crushing the power of that Delphic cult which had not only created the Peloponnesian War, but was the root of the doom which struck Greece once Plato's faction had been outflanked by the same Macedonian interests which were to plot the attempted assassination of Alexander the Great. However, by destroying the center of evil then based in the former maritime power of the evil cult of ancient Tyre, Alexander had crippled the cause of the oligarchical system until the aftermath of the Second Punic War: the formation of the Roman Empire was established by a pact struck on the Isle of Capri, between the priests of the cult of Mithra and the future Augustus Caesar. Capri was, thereafter, sacred to the person of the Roman emperors, up to about A.D. 500, when that and related territories were assigned to monastic orders. The deaths of Cicero, and, later, the great scientists the Platonic scholar Eratosthenes of Egypt and his associate Archimedes of Syracuse, mark out an interval of a history of rising Roman imperial rule and ruin coincident with the decline of the culture of the Mediterranean for centuries to come.

A Great Change Comes for Africa   45

The Peloponnesian War, orchestrated by the cult of Delphi, pitted the opposing mercantile-imperialist parties of Athens and Sparta in a battle over monetary primacy, leading to their common ruin.

since the Delphi-steered common ruin of the opposing mercantile-imperialist parties of Athens and Sparta in the infamous Peloponnesian War.

All known monetarist systems, imperialist ones most notably, as typified by those bandits of Wall Street and London controlling the mind of U.S. President Barack Obama up to this instant of writing, are intrinsically usurious, and hence parasitical. They are also apparently insane in their essential characteristics. All supranational efforts at "globalization," such as the London-steered, supranational agencies currently still controlling their present U.S. puppet, President Barack Obama, are now implicitly doomed to self-induced collapse during some uncertain date of the time during the weeks and months immediately ahead: unless President Obama were to dump the wretched pack of Larry Summers and the Behavioral psychologists shaping the President's economic policies of mismanagement at the present moment of writing. This onrushing doom will soon descend upon this entire planet, unless a timely, and seemingly radical change in essential policies is made soon.

For the foregoing reasons, we must say, that it is the intrinsically parasitical characteristic of all monetarist systems in history, which underlies those periodic collapses of entire social-political systems, which have characterized the span from birth to collapse of each such system in its turn.

So, in relevant past history, the imperial parasites have died, one by one, but have been usually replaced, as by a new master to replace the old, a new master whose behavior has been based on what is known to relevant historians as that same, oligarchical principle which led to the point of the demise of the predecessor. So, unfortunately, throughout known European history to date, like Asian empires before that, the demise of one parasite has usually led to its more or less early replacement by another blood-sucking successor. So, each such foolish system has died of a wave of starvation and related death in its time. In each case, the collapse had been triggered by the effects of the accumulated despoiling of its appointed prey, a collapse like that of both the presently collapsing physical economies of the U.S.A. and all Europe today.

Throughout the history of those cases of imperialism to which I have referred implicitly, here thus far, the underlying characteristic of empire has been monetary. In the case of European imperialisms, the empire was based, on the one hand, in its strategic maritime power respecting both commerce and control of the use of money by international organizations which held local forms of government as their colonies. The case of the Peloponnesian War is a prime illustration of this, as was true of Tyre prior to Alexander the Great, and Carthage prior to the close of Rome's Second Punic War.

Similarly, since the time that the rising monetarist power of Venice had superseded what had been the dominant role of Byzantium, since that decline of the imperial power of Byzantium which became conspicuous circa A.D. 1000-66, all expressions of European monetarist imperialism since then, to the present date, have been based upon the always continuing core of the Venetian financier oligarchy which rose to power in western Europe through its exploiting the weakening of the power of Byzantium in respect to the west and in the Middle East. The collapse of the power of Byzantium and rise of the power of Venice, led from the medieval tyranny of the feudal House of Anjou, into the emergence of the House of Habsburg's reign in Sicily and Spain. The weakening of the Habsburg power, in the course of the religious warfare of the A.D. 1492-1648 interval, led, in turn, to the rise of the present imperial period of the role of Venice in the specific Anglo-Dutch Liberal design of imperial financier oligarchy in northern Europe, as extended throughout the world at the present moment of writing this report.

The British Empire of today, which is the only world empire presently, is not a power of a sovereign nation, but of the slime-mold-like monetarist system of a financier imperialism. This characteristic of that system, is the axiomatic root of the onrushing destruction of civilization globally, today. As we must now echo the ancient Marcus Cato's, *"Carthargo delenda est."*[5]

The continuing decline of the Habsburgs' imperial power, during, and since the 1492-1648 period of religious warfare within Europe, was the key to the character of its successor. The successor was that rise of the Anglo-Dutch imperialism which was spawned by the Venetian financier circles associated with Paolo Sarpi. That latter formation, the Liberalism of Sarpi, is the present-day expression of that Venetian hand which holds the reins of that grim reaper now riding the backs of the London and Wall Street financier predators of the present instant. Thus, the current British political class and much of that of our own U.S.A., are nothing much more than chiefly, the ill-fated errand-boys of a British-centered imperium whose presently reigning, satanic soul, finds its ancestral home athwart not so much the canals of Venice, as flowing from the sewers native to the modern Venetian style in monetarist psyches.

The Roots of the American System

The best-designed defense of a sovereign nation against such Venetian-style international pirates, so far, has been found in the struggle for independence in our own United States. For that same reason, the principal target of hatred by that British Empire cast in the present version of the Venetian predatory, monetarist tradition, has been that movement of independence which arose within the English colonies of North America, a movement which arose first in Massachusetts, until the British acts of its repression during 1688-89, and, then, arose afresh, Phoenix-like, among such successors of the Massachusetts Winthrops and Mathers as, most no-

tably, the followers of Gottfried Leibniz associated with Benjamin Franklin.[6]

Franklin, who became not only a follower of what had been the great intellectual leaders of Massachusetts and Pennsylvania, such as Massachusetts' Cotton Mather and the circles of James Logan in Pennsylvania,[7] also enriched his intellectual inheritance from them by aid of intervention on his behalf by such Europeans as Germany's great Eighteenth-century mathematician Abraham Kästner, the same Kästner who guided the pair of founders of that Eighteenth-century European renaissance which was centered on the great modern Platonic figures of Gotthold Lessing and Moses Mendelssohn and their followers.

It was the legacy of the pre-1789 Classical movement centered on the roles of the circles of Kästner, Lessing, and Moses Mendelssohn, which had supplied the European core of the inspiration for, and support of the creation and defense of our own Federal republic. It was the work of Gottfried Leibniz which served, through channels such as those of Benjamin Franklin's sometime host, Professor Abraham Kästner, at Göttingen, as the scientific knowledge upon which the constitutional form of our anti-Locke, anti-British imperialist, American System of political-economy was premised.

So, it was this heritage of the founders of our own republic, including such students of Leibniz's work as Alexander Hamilton, which created the novel achievement of that anti-monetarist, American System of political-economy which is the core of the design for the U.S.A. Federal Constitution.

Hamilton, in particular, had been faced with the fact that the U.S. banks of the respective former colonies had been virtually bankrupted by the debts accumulated in the fighting of the battles for freedom from the British tyrant. This consideration led to the crafting of the U.S. Federal Constitution; only a perfect union of a single republic, as defined as the supreme constitutional law embodied within the Preamble of that Federal Constitution, could take the needed defensive measures required to preserve what the young American nation had gained from war against the brutish Liberal oppressor.[8]

---

5. "Carthage is to be destroyed."

6. Cf. H. Graham Lowry, *How the Nation Was Won: America's Untold Story* EPUB Kindle PDF (Washington, D.C.: Executive Intelligence Review, 1988).

7. Ibid.

8. The relevant American apologists for the treason directed from London, were customarily hysterical in their denial of the fact that the

This Russian website, reporting on the July 10, 2008 conference in Modena, Italy, emphasizes the role of Russian participants. The Modena Declaration, while delphically echoing many of LaRouche's policies, perniciously posits that a New Bretton Woods system would include "a new currency or basket of currencies (not necessarily limited to the U.S. dollar)." As LaRouche emphasizes in this paper, however, the dollar system must be sustained—on a Hamiltonian basis—if there is to be hope for recovery of any of the world's nations.

Our Anti-American Opponents

There are, of course, opposing, but wrong views of this matter among some Europeans today; but, such views are essentially an expression of either the illiteracy among many Europeans respecting both the economic and historical-cultural realities of modern, globally extended European civilization, or are the witting frauds served by such corrupted individuals as the Jonathan Tennenbaum and his present associates, who played a leading witting role, either directly, or indirectly, in concocting the political fraud foisted upon the notable Russian and other participants at Modena.

It is important, strategically, to emphasize this role of the Modena meeting here and now, because of its contribution to the global effect of temporarily misleading the Russian representatives to support that Modena scheme, since that hoax, pulled off there, disoriented the Russians' outlook sufficiently to have impaired his-

---

Preamble of the U.S. Federal Constitution is its most fundamental principle of law. Similarly, these implicitly treasonous scoundrels insist, contrary to all reason, that the U.S. Constitution is a product of that consummately evil promoter of slavery, John Locke.

torical U.S.-Russia relations significantly since that time, relations which are of presently crucial importance not only for Russia and the U.S.A. respectively, but the world as a whole. In large part, it was the fraud contributed by Tennenbaum, as a flagrantly apostate former scientific associate of mine, for the occasion of that meeting, which was employed to mislead the members of the Russian delegation, and others, at that Modena meeting.

That hoax, thus, has a certain unfinished history all its own.

Harry S Truman's Own Hoax

In the actual proceedings of the famous Bretton Woods conference of 1944, President Franklin Roosevelt had intervened to prevent the insertion of the pro-fascist, 1937, Berlin scheme of Britain's John Maynard Keynes into the 1944 Bretton Woods agreements. However, on the day following the death of Franklin Roosevelt, on April 13, 1945, the new President, Harry S Truman, tore up the most crucial strategic elements of Franklin Roosevelt's entire post-war policy, including the Bretton Woods policy, and brought in both Keynes' monetarist swindle and the related colonialist and other imperialist schemes of Britain's Winston Churchill et al. The so-called "Cold War" launched by the personal initiative of Winston Churchill at the close of the 1939-1945 general war against Hitler and Japan, was entirely a creation of the formerly fascist, British Empire, and its Wall Street, often formerly Hitler-loving figures, such as the circles of Averell Harriman flunky Prescott Bush, which came to control the U.S. Truman administration of 1945-1953.

In that sense, the formerly fascist, anti-Roosevelt forces associated with such as Averell Harriman and the J.P. Morgan interests, and with the circles of the larcenous Goldman Sachs today, went back to the British Liberals' old, formerly fascist ways, as they have acted similarly in the aftermath of July 25, 2007 now.

This virtually treasonous action by Truman, should not be seen as surprising to any competent historian today, from the Harry Truman whose nomination for Vice-President had been foisted on Roosevelt by right-wing Congressional and related forces' attempted blackmail at the 1944 Democratic convention. Truman was on record as closely associated with those U.S.

Wall Street interests, such as the Prescott Bush, serving the Averell Harriman of Brown Brothers Harriman, who had acted in concert with the head of the Bank of England, Montagu Norman, either to put Adolf Hitler into power in Germany or to exhibit kindred, "right wing" inclinations. It was only after the Japan attack on Pearl Harbor, that the Wall Street gang which had backed both Mussolini and Hitler during most of the 1920s and 1930s, reluctantly, and only temporarily, mended their conduct, until President Roosevelt's death let them loose to play in the customarily treasonous ways of such among their predecessors, as the British Foreign Office agent Aaron Burr.[9]

Harry Truman tore up FDR's post-war policies, in favor of the imperial schemes of Britain's Winston Churchill and John Maynard Keynes.

to be condemned, was that not only did he act, in implicitly treasonous expressions of hatred of President Franklin Roosevelt, hatred expressed by his moving to defend a mass-murderous scheme of wars and genocides which his promotion of the cause of Anglo-Dutch financier imperialism actually caused up to the present time; but, it was Truman's contribution to the promotion of the imperialist system of monetarism inherent in Keynes' 1937 Nazi-Germany edition of his **General Theory**, which Truman's defense of Keynes' anti-Franklin Roosevelt, anti-U.S.A., Bretton Woods proposal, did, in fact, support.

The effects of Truman's virtual treason have come in three successive, general phases since that time.

I explain:

First, consider President Truman's own actions as President. This set of actions, by him, was predominantly threefold, as follows. These provided the foundation for other equally contemptible actions of high-ranking officials and interests later.

In his initial moral crime as President, which was done in combination with his guidance by Winston Churchill, he cancelled President Franklin Roosevelt's anti-Keynesian design for a post-war, anti-colonialist system of physical-economic development of the world at large, with Roosevelt's special emphasis on universal eradication of colonial and kindred forms of imperialist subjugation. Truman snuffed out Roosevelt's intention, sending the U.S. economy careening into the deep recession of 1948.

Truman's second violation, that to similar effect, was to wreck the economic prospect which Roosevelt had intended to bring into being through maintaining the peacetime economic potential of the great war-machine which had been built up for the war, but which he intended to reorient to the physical-economic build-up

In viewing those facts, and they are solid facts, we must take into account the present-day effects of the radical change in U.S. strategic and economic policies which Truman's actions of April 13, 1945 had brought about. The case of the referenced hoax pulled off at Modena, Italy, is a relevant point of reference under present international circumstances.[10]

Among the other specific counts of criminality for which deceased Harry Truman's poor soul might expect

---

9. Prescott Bush was, at that time, a leading figure of the Wall Street firm of Brown Brothers Harriman, a Wall Street extension of the London firm of leading creator of the Hitler regime in Germany, the Montagu Norman who deployed his flunky Hjalmar Schacht as the key promoter of the Hitler regime through the channels of the Basel, Switzerland-based Bank for International Settlements (BIS). Prescott Bush, acting in this capacity, moved funds controlled by Brown Brothers Harriman to fund Adolf Hitler's way out of bankruptcy, just in time to bring Hitler into power in Germany. Subsequent history shows both the relevant son and grandson of Prescott Bush, as U.S. Presidents, to have been fully in that branch of British imperial and Wall Street traditions.

10. Had Tennenbaum, therefore, become a fascist? No. I can only be certain that he was merely corrupted, acting under the risk that his wife might have made his life thoroughly, and perpetually miserable, had he not consented to turn scoundrel for that occasion.

of the nations of the world, especially the victims of British and comparable forms of colonial and semi-colonial bondage. Truman turned the U.S. back to support of British imperialism, by giving full support to his crony Churchill in restoring the British, Dutch, and French empires, in particular, or, as in the case of India, dividing it and subjugating it to conditionalities-in-fact. This turn in U.S. policy was the direct cause for the serious economic recession of 1946-1948 in the U.S.A. under the Truman Presidency.

The head of the British East India Company operations, Lord Shelburne, had adopted the method of the Roman Emperor Julian the Apostate, by putting the religious constituencies of his subjects at one another's throats, even into wars. That is the British imperial method still today, as under the imperial Sykes-Picot system of Arab-versus-Arab and Arab-versus-Jew in the Middle East presently.

The third step by Truman, was his complicity with Churchill in their support of so-called "pacifist" Bertrand Russell's launching the intention for a "preventive nuclear war" against a Soviet Union which had had no malice against the United States at that time. This British imperialist policy did have the full support of those Wall Street-centered, fascist sympathizers which had dominated the United States of the 1920s, and had been a powerful, Wall Street-centered fascist political interest lurking at President Roosevelt's back even during the war against Adolf Hitler.

The second general, post-Truman phase of the U.S. decline, began more than a decade after a disgusted U.S. establishment's dumping of Truman, in 1964, when, despite some initiatives of President Dwight Eisenhower, an intended long-term wrecking of the U.S. economy was expressed in the ruinous policies, such as the ruinous U.S. long war in Indo-China, intro-

President John Kennedy and Attorney General Robert Kennedy at the White House. The assassination of the President led quickly to the quagmire of the Indo-China War.

duced in the wake of the assassination of President John F. Kennedy.

Kennedy, with the support of two Five-Star Generals, had been committed to keeping the U.S.A. out of "a land war in Asia." The launching of that war, which was made possible by both the assassination of President Kennedy, and by President Johnson's fear that he was probably the next target of the London-centered, international forces behind Kennedy's death, led quickly to the Asian quagmire of an unnecessary and unwarranted Indo-China war, and to a wrecking of the U.S. through the domestic economic side-effects of that lunatic war.

That phase in the post-war pattern of U.S. affairs, was then continued as the later, 1968-1989, second stage of the continued ruin of the U.S. economy from within. This was the continuation of the post-Kennedy decline under, first, President Richard Nixon, and then, the outrightly criminal measures of wrecking of our economy and our national security under the 1975-1981 control of the Trilateral Commission represented by Zbigniew Brzezinski. From this set of implicitly treasonous trickery, our economy had never fully recovered, to the present day.

The third, and present, such post-Franklin Roosevelt phase in the U.S. economy, was launched with the combination of the major, depression-level, October 1987 "recession," after which the new Chairman of the Federal Reserve System, Alan Greenspan, and his implicitly criminal financial methods, brought us into the presently escalating, global general breakdown-crisis.

During the closing interval of Chairman Alan Greenspan's reign over the mad wrecking of our banking system, we experienced the qualitative change to the present new phase, which took over with the post-July 2007 eruption of the presently accelerating, worldwide general breakdown-crisis of the entire world economy.

The Present State of Crisis

The nature of the immediately available remedies for the present state of crisis, is defined by the notion of law of bankruptcy established, as the remedy against the evil of debtors prisons, by U.S. bankruptcy law. Two considerations have now come into play. We must now put the U.S. financial system into the forms of reorganization in bankruptcy implicit in our Federal Constitution. We must defend our republic, and also the world at large, from the threatened, planetary new dark age which is implicit in what has recently been, the present, virtually criminal role which had been performed by the slimy successor to Robert Rubin as Treasury Secretary, Larry Summers, in crafting a destruction of the U.S. banking system through destroying the Glass-Steagall law.

At the time of my international webcast of July 25, 2007, and the several weeks immediately following, the internal U.S. crisis which first broke out three days after that webcast, could have been brought under control. It was chiefly actions of leading circles within the U.S. Congress, as illustrated by the actions of Senator Christopher Dodd and Representative Barney Frank, which prevented those remedies from being adopted. Those ruinous actions which were laundered through the U.S. Congress under Speaker Nancy Pelosi, and through the U.S. George W. Bush administration, set into motion the presently threatened breakdown-crisis of not only the U.S.A. and the United Kingdom, but, now, the entire planet. For that, those persons must assume a full burden of shame.

Until the current U.S. President, Barack Obama, made his ill-fated pilgrimage to Buckingham Palace, to stand next to the wicked little Queen and her evil consort, there was hope that the lunacy and virtual criminality of the departed George W. Bush, would be brought to an end by a "non-Bush" President. Now, our citizens' hopes are being crushed, as the situation now is already far worse than anything which had occurred while the thoroughly ruinous, and disgusting President Bush was still in office.

So, for the moment, the policies of the new President have been controlled by the frankly fascist policies, in some part "neo-Nazi" social and population policies of the pack of "Behaviorist" psychologists such as Peter R. Orszag, whose social policies in health care and related matters are already frank copies of the social policies, including that of death-acceleration of the sick and elderly, which were set into motion in Sep-

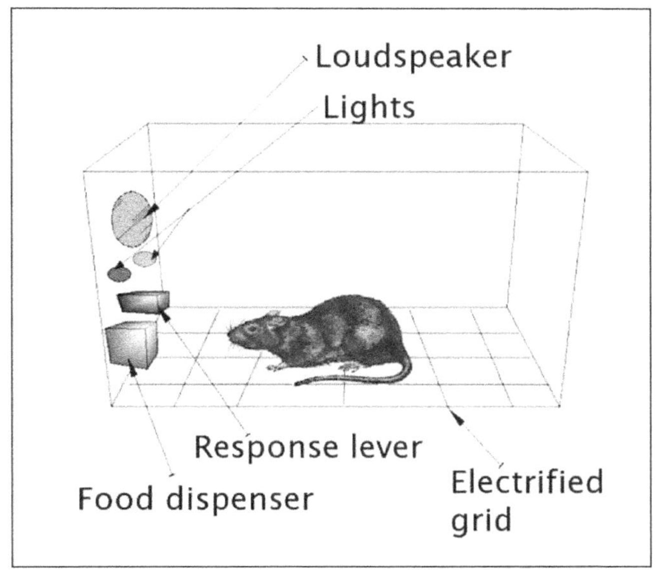

GNU Free Documentation License

A pack of professed "behaviorist economists" is shaping President Obama's economic policies, and the population's response to them, just as behaviorist psychologists "teach" the rat in a Skinner Box to do what his controllers want him to do.

tember 1939 by the Nazi Adolf Hitler regime which had been put into power in Germany by the Bank of England.

However, even now, there are remedies for even those morally terrible crimes which Summers and Orszag typify in U.S. national policies; but, they are remedies which will not exist for us unless, and until Larry Summers and his "Behaviorist" accomplices are turned over, very soon, for the ministrations of the relevant political rubbish collectors, when they might be dumped, for the edification of the public, as if on the pavements of the sidewalk facing the Executive Mansion. Nonetheless, that said, well-defined optional remedies for both our republic, and the world, still, presently exist. That unique set of remedies is now our subject here.

I. A Credit-System Versus The Monetarist System

In the case of any business enterprise, or national economy, such as the governments of the U.S.A., or Europe today, which is led by ostensibly qualified people, but which is in stubborn decline, the qualified expert's foremost hypothesis will be, that the reason he, or she, as an outsider has been brought in, is, in fact, that the root of that drift toward failure is a product of adherence to "management methods," or goals, which the leadership of that firm defends, as if axiomatically not the cause of the problem. The qualified outsider who pries into sacred territory in that way, can often be shown to have adopted the correct investigative hypothesis some time near to, even prior to the outset of that investigation.

Any competent presentation of proposed remedies cohering with my own exceptionally successful experience as an economic forecaster, must be situated by reference to the starting-point of a few autobiographical references, references premised upon the working principle, that the cause of disasters of empires, nations, or other matured enterprises, lies somewhere among policies, or systemic misperceptions which those organizations have adopted as if they were the most treasured secrets of their traditions, or, simply, what had been their choice of a presumed road to success.

In such matters, a prudent assumption is that popular opinion, even when it is official, is usually wrong. Since my first general economic forecast for the U.S. economy, back in Summer of 1956, my valid forecast, of a probable fall of the U.S.A. into a deep recession by February-March 1957, was unique among the professional and business circles with which I was associated. My successful forecast saw the cause of the problem as lying in both the dogmas of the chief economic advisor to the administration of President Eisenhower, Arthur Burns, and the skyrocketing influence of the dupes of schemes more or less consistent with the radically positivist ways of thinking typified by the hysterically incompetent von Neumann-Morgenstern "theory of games."[11]

The uttering of "Our tradition is," often proves, thus, to be tantamount to the signing of an economic suicide-note by either a business enterprise, or a government, even a leading government. Otherwise, they would not be clinging so stubbornly to what they have regarded as their "tried and tested," but actually failed principles.[12] Once that aspect of the facts before us is made clear, the rest of the matter flows, not without some difficulties for today's student, but, otherwise, an effort pursued in a more appropriate direction.

No factor in policy-shaping of the United States has been as important in its role of bringing on the presently recent five decades of decline, and imminently threatened disintegration of the economies of both Europe and our United States, as the adoption of impassioned devotion to the belief that the secret of U.S. progress lies in devotion to the faith in the anti-Alexander Hamilton, anti-Franklin Roosevelt cult of "free trade," that cult of both Adam Smith and his avowed devotee Karl Marx.

That said: those discoveries which I have made which led to my, so far, decades-long, relatively unique successes in long-term forecasting, have been a method which can be approached by focusing attention less upon my opponents' often treasured superficial appearances, than on either the sometimes brutal fact of either their frank incompetence, or, in other cases, their simply inevitable lack of effectiveness. The needed approach to such matters may be launched, often, through attention to, chiefly, what should be recognized as some rather elementary historical facts. I follow just that historical approach in the course of this present and following chapters of this report.

It is often a most challenging proposition, emotionally, to attempt to understand the reasons for, and correction of a detected deficiency shown by relevant specialists and others in this matter. In such cases, the strain comes often in the form of the necessity of forcing even prominent economists, or other specialists, to abandon deeply embedded commitment to the more commonplace, but mistaken, and strongly held assumptions, especially those held among reluctant influentials with either advanced qualities of professional backgrounds or merely raw political influence.

The simpler fact to be considered in considering the

---

11. John v. Neumann and Oskar Morgenstern, **Theory of Games & Economic Behavior**, 3rd ed. (Princeton, N.J.: Princeton, 1953). My examination of their work was the result of prompting by my January 1948 encounter with a pre-publication, reviewer's edition of Norbert Wiener's savage, quackish denial of the existence of human creativity, in his **Cybernetics**. It was this quackery which had prompted David Hilbert to throw, first, radically positivist Bertrand Russell dupe Norbert Wiener, and, later, Russell devotee John von Neumann, out of his Göttingen program, on clearly valid charges of vicious forms of scientific incompetence. This had prompted what became my own lifelong devotion to the subject of the role of creativity in the domain of physical economy. This became the basis for my exceptional advantage as a long-range economic forecaster.

12. The reader must not overlook the fact, that a government may successfully defend a policy by which it is ruining itself, with the obvious result that the defeated opponent of that same policy is being vindicated. Which role would you prefer for yourself? You may be able to guess my choice.

disputes among forecasters lately, is, that my own repeated accomplishments as an advocate of what Alexander Hamilton christened as *The American System of political-economy*, have been the basis for my, speaking relatively, extraordinarily successful role in what might be termed "long-range forecasting;" whereas, what might be fairly named as the more popular European, or U.S., "brand X" varieties, have never really succeeded for longer than the relatively short life of "guesstimates" which may appear to have been valid, even briefly triumphant, but were disastrous over longer than relatively brief intervals of local history. Meanwhile, my authority in this field of practice has been repeatedly demonstrated to have been, generally, both unique, and repeatedly successful over the relatively long term, in respect to the relevant, generally known history of this subject thus far.

Thus, the core of my required mission in this report, is to contribute to making clear some of the most relevant, more readily accessible, practical issues of successful, versus failed forms of forecasting.

Just so, as throughout the time since the death of President Franklin Roosevelt, there were a number of lapses of time during which the very policies which were the causes of the next serious economic crisis, were those which had appeared to the credulous to have been successful. Their saddening error to be recognized, was that those who were duped temporarily into relative euphoria, were confident that their goal, the "pea" of the charlatan's game, would be found under the shell toward which they were pointing. The shell was there, indeed, as they insisted on that fact as proof of their argument; but, as to what was waiting, or not, under that shell, that was a different matter. So the momentary euphoria of the credulous paled into sadness, as they turned to walk away, poorer, but, unfortunately, usually, no wiser. So, the preaching of the doctrine of reporting "good news" was, almost invariably, a "suckers' game," a game which the temporarily wounded, but habituated sucker of the previous time, would move, confidently, to play again on the next occasion. But, it was the same with the effect of the choice of previous candidate, or political quack-remedy which they bought into during the preceding time![13]

So, we say to the less credulous, and more prudent, that while I distinguish the relatively limited authority of attractive approximations, from the, contrary, scientifically deep, epistemological issues of physical science, it is the deeper, longer-range issues which must be ultimately taken into account in the present crisis, as must always be done for successful forecasting over the crucial, longer term of two or more generations ahead. *It is not statistics that determine the future, but policies.*

However, those considerations taken into account, the most prevalent cause of failures of economists and leading political figures, alike, is that they show no working comprehension of that one great principle which actually distinguishes man from the apes.

Percy Shelley, Again

The most consequential fact of that matter, is, that a lack of a manifest comprehension of the role of creative processes in one's own mental development, or, in that of others, does not signify that creative potential itself does not exist, nor that it does not occasionally manifest itself even in the relatively unwitting person. Rather, it can be observed as manifest in persons who, as Shelley made a similar warning in the concluding paragraph of his **A Defence of Poetry**, often have no comprehension of the way in which the products of their own exceptional moments of genuinely creative impulse actually worked successfully, even if they lacked any deeper insight into how that success had been generated within them. As that paragraph from Shelley should be taken as implying, the usual failure of economists, for example, is not that the actual power of creativity does not exist in our species generally, but that it has been often suppressed, even brutally, in the combined education and related development among most relevant persons and institutions today.

For example.

It was more or less well known, in those past times, such as two or more generations ago, when the subject of Classical, rather than empiricist modes in education was still treated as serious business, that in the mission of promoting creativity in students, or other persons, it was of crucial importance that the teacher, or other relevant person, concentrate on attempting to provoke and recognize the symptoms of a creative impulse in, for example, the student, and not to depart that moment which that just freshly expressed impulse represented,

---

13. Such as the swindle called "infrastructure" which the New York Mayor was peddling, temporarily, on behalf of the Rockefeller Foundation.

The Charlestown Navy Yard in 1921. Not many years later, a young Lyndon LaRouche visited the yard, noting the fascinating role of physical geometry in the supporting structures there—such as strategically placed holes that make the structure more stable. The Eiffel Tower in Paris illustrates the same point: the failure of axiomatic assumptions of Euclidean geometry.

without focusing the relevant persons', or classroom's attention on the "location" of the exactly expressed location and nature of the creative impulse which the student had exhibited in passing.

This phenomenon, the manifestation of that power of creativity which does not exist in any beast, but only among human individuals, is the essential consideration in all consideration of the nature and the outcome of physical-economic processes. All competent treatment of the subject of economy as a matter of science, hangs entirely on that specific consideration which today's accounting profession, for example, does not actually recognize. It is on that principle of creativity, that the continued existence of a civilized existence of mankind depends.

While the evidence which constitutes proof of those facts, is clear in its own right, the overriding fact is, that, for our specific purposes here, on this occasion, it is essential that we come to a common understanding of the "how" and "why" of the uniqueness, to date, of the role of creativity in bringing about my own rather striking successes in this aspect of economic forecasting. Otherwise, without that emphasis, discussion of the place of creativity in economic forecasting lacks its most essential expression for the benefit of society, its intentionally functional, rather than a "happenstance" quality.

My Own Experience

Briefly, as I have reported on earlier occasions, in my own development of creativity in myself, we have the following.

Insofar as I can account now for the roots of my success, relative to what might appear to be rival opinion-making in this profession of economic studies, in my first awareness that I had a significantly "different view" of the matter of creativity than was proposed in the secondary and university experiences to which I was exposed during adolescence and young adulthood. Awareness of this fact first came to me during the first secondary-school class in plane geometry, in which I rejected the axiomatic, *a-priori* assumptions of that teaching. My rejection had been prompted largely by my prior studies of construction-in-progress at the nearby Charlestown U.S. Navy Yard, which had demonstrated, for me, the physically efficient, unique role of *physical geometry* in design of supporting structures. The case of the Eiffel Tower in Paris illustrates that importance of relying on physical geometry, rather than Euclidean geometry. The axiomatic (e.g., *a-priori*) assumptions of Euclidean geometry are intrinsically false.

It is relevant here, that my rejection of secondary school geometry, and of some other, related matters, matters which I encountered, chiefly, in my exposure to the standard teaching of mathematics and physical science at the institutions to which I was exposed, impelled me, on this account, from early adolescence on, into an increasingly voracious appetite for such works of Leibniz as I could find in English translation. In my later adolescent years, I chose Immanuel Kant as the case of a relevant adversary of Leibniz who was chosen by me for making comparisons bearing upon the ontological issues so posed by such a form of dialogue, which I conducted within me, in a back-and-forth exploration of more and more of the accessible work-product of each of those two persons.

Eventually, this led, I would say inevitably, or, perhaps according to an "hereditary" principle like that linking seed to plant, to my crucial insight into the significance of Bernhard Riemann's 1854 habilitation dissertation, an insight which came upon me about a hundred years after that presentation by him; it came to me, like an epiphany, so to speak, at the beginning of 1953.

At the same time, my exposure to the role of innovation of design in the production-process, was significantly the product of questions posed to me in the practical context of my family circumstances, that as combined with my fascination with Classical English poetry. These combined, ostensibly dissimilar influences, drove me more and more deeply into emphasis on the role of actually creative innovation in the production of wealth, and into my increasing emphasis on the distinction between ordinary sorts of cleverness in craftsmanship, and the need to pinpoint the distinction of special quality of the craftsmanship which is specific to the actual role of discovery and use of universal principles, such as those of physical science, but also Classical composition in the tradition of Johann Sebastian Bach.

I think it was therefore almost inevitable, that that process would bring me to Bernhard Riemann's absolutely revolutionary transformation of the definition of physical-scientific method in his 1854 habilitation dissertation. For similar reasons, in my work as a practicing consultant, I came to abhor what I recognized as the intrinsic incompetence of the use of more or less standard forms of accounting practice and of customary statistical methods in the practices of forecasting.

Today, reviewing my life's larger experience from the standpoint of long-standing, recurring disputes over the nature and goals of scientific method, the attempt to enable even accomplished scientists to achieve what might be termed "a direct insight" into creativity as such, is the most challenging task to be presented even to a majority among leading scientists known to me today, and, generally speaking, far more difficult today than two decades earlier.[14] Today's professionals simply give up the attempt much quicker than those professionals of two or three decades ago would have done. Only the degree of impassioned concern which the presently skyrocketing, global economic crisis evokes, could now prompt the broader kind of commitment which would bring insight into the ontological character of human creativity per se.

The 'Basement Project'

As part of exactly that attempt, there came a time, the larger part of a decade ago, when I launched what became known among my associates as "The Basement Project," in working groups situated in the premises where my office was located.[15] This project has been conducted, chiefly, by the qualified members of those teams themselves, persons selected chiefly from what appeared to be matured and dedicated young minds in their twenties. These research projects covered a span of time equivalent to about four semesters added to their education, a period of working, thoroughly, systemically, through the discoveries of Johannes Kepler and the principal work of Gauss, covering, initially, replication of Kepler's uniquely original discovery of the universal principle of gravitation, the latter as presented in his **The Harmonies of the World**.

This experience has lain the grounds for those students' treatment of the more fundamental issues associ-

---

14. There is, perhaps, no more convincing demonstration of that problem than considering the number of otherwise credible professors in physical-science fields who will argue the nonsensical assertion that Sir Isaac Newton had discovered the principal of gravitation, rather than the actual discoverer, Johannes Kepler. Even most scientists believe what they wish to be overheard believing in such cases, even when the evidence to the contrary is overwhelming. So much for "peer review" in modern houses of academic prostitution!.

15. This project was launched in response to university campus phenomena which I located in the setting of the 1999-2000 Presidential election-campaign. An educational program launched in California, in response to these phenomena of that time, preceded the programs which I later launched on the East Coast. When I look back to the Year 2000, and then compare the much poorer quality of persons of a comparable age-group, after the effects of MySpace, Facebook, Twitter, etc., today, we are forced to recognize how deep and broad have been the cultural pessimism and loss of creative intellectual potential among young adults during the eight years of the President George W. Bush, Jr. administration.

ated with the work of Bernhard Riemann and such among his most notable followers, as Max Planck, Albert Einstein, and Academician V. I. Vernadsky.

The goal of this continuing program into the domain of Riemannian physical science, in a manner similar to that of an earlier program in the systemically progressive work of Carl F. Gauss, has been aimed to set a standard of practice for a comparable, currently ongoing work in the combined territory of the discoveries of Bernhard Riemann and such successors as Max Planck, and in the crucial role of Albert Einstein, figures which exemplify the center of the resistance to the morbid decadence of the successive development of positivist theology by such as Ernst Mach and the markedly satanic Bertrand Russell. My own focus, and that of my young associates in this matter, has been the implications of this for a science of physical economy.

There, the main body of that still ongoing work stands in continuing progress today.

Any competent teaching and practice of a science of political economy, in the realities of today's world, must be essentially, as Academician V.I. Vernadsky has shown, a branch subsuming the Riemannian physical bio-chemistry of human voluntary intervention into shaping the direction of development of man's relationship to the universe. This proceeds, as it must, with fundamental emphasis on both the opening two paragraphs and closing sentence of Riemann's 1854 habilitation dissertation. That is to say, that without Kepler, Leibniz, and Riemann (most notably), and such successors of Riemann as Max Planck, Albert Einstein and Academician V.I. Vernadsky, no competent training in a professional treatment of economics could be provided for today's presently crisis-ridden, global circumstances.

That is also to emphasize, that, although a significant minority among practicing economists in, for example, Europe and the Americas, are both competent and important, even often indispensable, in those aspects of the matter of what they practice as economics, almost none of them, even of the best practitioners, get into the underlying physical-scientific essentials of that subject-matter. Almost—but not absolutely—all, even among the relative best, lack a systemic comprehension of the most crucial issues underlying the search for remedies for the presently accelerating, global breakdown-crisis of the entire world's economy. Much of the source of their failures on this account, is their more or less militant, even bald ignorance of even the functional rudiments of the history of the American System of political-economy. Such is the subject of the challenge which we are addressing in this present location.

Specifically, we are faced with the incompetence on the subject of the U.S. Constitution and the American System of political-economy, which is rampant today among not only European, but also most relevant American academics and political figures. Even Americans have been "brainwashed," academically, into attacking the American System from the standpoint of the axiomatic presumptions of the British East India Company's ideologues, such as Adam Smith and Jeremy Bentham's crew, rather than considering the proofs of the absurdity of the principal assumptions of the British imperialist system of thought. Much of this brainwashing has depended less on ignorance of that subject, that on the popularity of outright lies.

The most prevalent fault among these exceptional cases of the relatively most competent, practicing professionals among today's economists, is that since nearly all notable such are usually gainfully employed in that profession, they must have tended to concentrate their professional exertions on the requirements imposed upon them by those institutions which have trained them, or by clients who purchase their wares, and, thus, they tend to concentrate on the "bread-and-butter" issues of producing the product which that market for their services had demanded, rather than the imperatives of the relevant science itself.[16] Nonetheless, when a crisis like the present one strikes, serious economists' suspicions are aroused.

It is my own experience, that the best hope for the future of the economics profession, is that development which occurs when "consumers" of that product, such as members of our Congress or of European parliaments, become much wiser than they are today. It is clear, that, when, as the intelligence of their clientele's choice of appetites is improved, the economists themselves will tend to adapt to the impassioned demands of a better-informed, and angry market composed of their clienteles.

In the meanwhile, prudent professionals confronted

---

16. Often the public suffers from the design of the product it has chosen by the standards which pass for those of popular taste, such as expressed by popular acclaim for the launching and conduct of foolish wars, or the systemic degeneration of the personality of the habitual user of cannabis.

with the present crisis, are now advised, urgently, to make themselves familiar, here and now, with a fair approximation of the appropriate expertise which is expressed in this, my present report.

The Essential Role of Creativity

The "basement program," to which I referred above, was coupled, in an intentionally functional way, with a Classical-musical program pivoted, initially, on what I had already selected as J.S. Bach's motet **Jesu, meine Freude**. My principal motive in sponsoring such a program within the setting of a political-action association and its science educational program, was premised on locating the root of that individual creativity which is also expressed within the domains of physical science. This means, most emphatically, a practice which depends on the type of a primary quality of principled expression of creativity, which is located essentially in the realm of Classical artistry, but certainly not in most so-called "popular entertainments" of today.

This is creativity, as expressed typically in the modes of Classical irony in poetry, and in, most emphatically, the principles of Johann Sebastian Bach, as these were faithfully served by strictly Classical composers in the Bach tradition of such as his own sons, as also by Joseph Haydn, by Wolfgang Mozart, by Ludwig Beethoven, and, so on, through Johannes Brahms. The image of Albert Einstein performing the violin in services at the great Jewish synagogue in pre-Hitler regime Berlin, is not irrelevant for study of the positive development of modern Germany and both its scientific and Classical cultural tradition under the pre-Hitler influences of the great modern Platonist Moses Mendelssohn and his extended family of relatives extended throughout much of the German-speaking world of music and fundamental progress in physical science.

For example: over six decades to date, I have returned repeatedly, as may be noted by readers here, to references to Percy Bysshe Shelley's work, especially his extraordinary **A Defence of Poetry**, especially the concluding paragraph of that composition. It is in the process of singing of Classical poetry, that we are best informed to point out the location within the human mind where the creative genius of all art and science are essentially rooted. It is the Classical mode of sung poetic counterpoint, as typified for modern languages by the work of Johann Sebastian Bach and his followers, through Johannes Brahms, which is the well-spring

from which the waters of creativity flow into the rivers and seas of Classical physical-scientific progress. From this we must secure the resulting increase of the productive powers of labor of mankind, per capita and per square kilometer of territory.

It is the loss of a rigorous practice of Classical modes of artistic composition and performance, which has been the characteristic expression of the moral and intellectual decadence which has gripped the trans-Atlantic community increasingly, since the time of the death of U.S. President Franklin Roosevelt on April 12, 1945. Much of the economic and other ruin of the nations of the trans-Atlantic community, in particular, has taken root in the vicious decadence of popular trends in artistic expressions, especially in the existentialist currents typified by the case of the 1950 **The Authoritarian Personality** of Theodor Adorno et al., and by its pro-fascist correlative, the Congress for Cultural Freedom (CCF).[17]

On this account, the fostering of the implicitly Satanic-dionysiac, so-called "existentialist" rituals promoted during the post-World War II period to date, as by that pro-Satanic Congress for Cultural Freedom, has been, in its time, a leading stimulant of the interdependent moral and physical-economic decay which grips the planet as a whole today.[18]

The somewhat extended, but otherwise summary remarks with which I have now, thus, opened this chapter of the main body of this report, now bring us to the following.

Two Contrasted Species of Life

The presently required remedies for our world's condition, now depend, and that absolutely, on the very early replacement of the present world monetary system by what I identify here as a credit-system, a credit-system as defined by the example of the U.S. Federal Constitution. The replacement must be in the form of a credit-system which is modeled upon the relevant provisions of the U.S. Federal Constitution, as I define that system and its application, in these pages.

In the course of this and the following chapters, the

---

17. I treat this relevant subject in the concluding portion of Chapter III.
18. This post-1945 corruption was not only an echo of the similar post-World War I moral breakdown, especially in Europe. The CCF and the publication of **The Authoritarian Personality** represented a more radical form of moral and intellectual depravity than the pattern of the emergence of European fascism during the 1920s and 1930s.

better informed reader will probably be shocked by a sense of *deja vu!*, when he or she reflects on the way the U.S.A.'s economy has often been viewed as differing little, in superficial ways, from seeming to be only a less demoralized complement to the process and model of physical economic-monetary systems of modern western Europe, especially since Spring 1968. When we consider this social phenomenon in its aspect as matters of economic policies of practice, it turns out, with even a fairly modest reflection on the facts of the matter, that the difference between the American System of political-economy and the usual European models appears to be, on the one side, like the contrast of mammals to marsupials, or even to monotremes: orders of life with some external similarities in the eyes of the chance observer, but what is an essentially mutually incompatible reproductive character among these orders.

Both mammals and marsupials are "animals," but they exist and reproduce according to different categories of principle, as the morally and scientifically superior American System differs from the relatively depraved, typical, British empire and its dominant role among the designs of European parliamentary models, and their monetary systems, or economic systems, still today.

The typical reader, including professional economists, must be reminded, repeatedly, that the subject here is not a matter of superficial similarities, or differences among credit systems and modern monetarist systems, but a matter of what are, respectively, systemically, "genetically" incompatible methods of *social-economic reproduction of what are, in principle, categorically different orders among species.*[19]

The essential similarity among the differing principal models of economies on the planet today, is that the subjects of both models are human beings; both kinds of modern societies are members of a species whose proper mode of social reproduction as living individuals, is expressed as that potential of true creativity which distinguishes all human beings from mere animals, that absolutely, *categorically*. That difference in types is located in the respective social-political-economic systems within which people have been enabled so far, in principle, to exercise, and therefore develop their inherent creative potential as human beings, either more or less freely or, even, as today's dionysiac,

---

19. No reference to the so-called British "upper classes" intended here.

"greenie" fanatics would have it, not at all.

Therefore, the crucial feature of our enterprise here could reach our goal for it, only as it is to be seen when we might contrast the fixed potential relative population-densities of the higher apes, for each case of any given environment, to the increase of the growth of density of a typical culture of the human population. The facts should inform us, quickly, that systemic differences in social organization taken into account, man, unlike the higher apes, is no mere animal. The facts also show, on the other hand, a strong taint of the monetarist legacy of the imperial system of European feudalism, in even the nominally sovereign European systems of today.

In brief, there is a distinct principle, a principle of human creativity, which separates the human individual, and his or her species, absolutely from all lower forms of life. Thus, speaking in pedagogically relevant terms, man is to mere animals, relatively speaking, as living processes and their specific products and by-products are to the inanimate domain.

Now consider the crucial paradox which all competent attempts at a definition of economics must solve:

Any relatively healthy form of human society, if it is actually progressing to higher levels of potential relative population-density, is always converging upon two principal kinds of freshly threatened general limitation upon both the increase and well-being of its population. The society's continued growth, even its continued existence, is bounded, negatively, on the one hand, by the limits implicit in its available environment; it is also bounded negatively, on the other hand, and at the same time, by its unavoidable tendency to outrun the types of limits to growth inherent in all animal species, the trend for a relatively large depletion of any environment, a depletion which must occur, unless we bring into play mankind's characteristic, *anti-entropic action*, which distinguishes mankind from all lower forms of life.

That distinction, is a more than offsetting factor of tendencies for, or combating depletion of the environment, by raising the level of that society's technology through actions in the forms expressed typically by a combined scientific and Classical cultural creativity, a creativity which, combined, is unique as being that power of our human species which sets our species apart from both the apes, and from the intentions of certain current policies and heads of state, such as today's intrinsically pro-fascist, intrinsically lying, "greenie" ideologies of the evil Prince Philip's World Wildlife Fund.

When those simple, but clear items of evidence are viewed from the vantage-point of contemporary physical science, we show, even in the appropriate terms of the physical chemistry of living processes generally, that the boundary presented to the maintenance of the present population-level of any case of human society, requires the society to raise both the level of adducible mean energy-flux density of its productive system, and to mobilize a defense of Classical humanist forms of cultural progress in science and arts, that progress as opposed to the accelerated rates of spread of dionysian forms of cultural depravity in Europe and the Americas, for example, today. This indispensable principle of progress is to be viewed, for purposes of definitions and comparisons, in terms of references to those physical bio-chemistries rooted in the present state of development of the notion of a periodic table.

Such a table must be read in terms of the relevance of the comparative standards of respectively distinct abiotic, biotic, and noëtic qualities of physical phase-spaces. These three standards are to be compared in terms of the anti-entropic relationship of living processes to abiotic, and noëtic to biotic. In order to avoid collapse through attrition, the ratio of the sheer mass of the Biosphere to Lithosphere must be increasing, and the ratio of Noösphere to Biosphere must also be increasing similarly, that both per capita and per square kilometer of the Earth's surface. *These requirements for physical-economic survival of our species, depend upon a process of continuing increase of the mean "energy-flux density" in society's mode of reproduction of its population.*[20] Without a present return to the tradi-

Courtesy of J. Gordon Edwards

The late J. Gordon Edwards, an entomologist, fought against Rachel Carson's lies, notably about the pesticide DDT. Here he is shown in Esquire *magazine, September 1971, eating a tablespoon of the chemical—a feat he repeated regularly, to emphasize the safety of the chemical. (He died at the ripe old age of 85.)*

tion of increasing the expression of ongoing increasing of the relative energy-flux density of production, per capita and per square kilometer of the Earth's surface, world society were presently committed to its own early doom, whatever the apparent, current state of financial affairs might otherwise seem to be.

Such are the most essential elements for consideration, in defining the relevant elements of *a science of physical economy.*[21]

The difference in systems is marked, today, by the fact that under a continued reign of monetarist systems, the entire planet is now doomed, in the immediate future, to a prolonged, and very deep plunge into a planet-wide "new dark age." *The crucial difference between our American System of political-economy, on the one hand, and European and other monetarist systems, on the other, is a qualitative difference in political-economic species, in which the former has the better power to survive, whereas the latter, under the present conditions of the world's presently reigning, monetarist system of London et al., does not—except as it has been inspired by the relatively most successful phases of U.S. world leadership in the quality of its economy.*

---

interactions subsumed by a common cluster of which a region of the Biosphere is composed. Decent people like good dogs, so much, that the characteristics of the dog populations of various regions of the planet reflect this human factor in the destiny of dog life. Dogs have been brought, thus, if by no choice of their own, into the dynamics of the higher domain of the Noösphere. Thus, have kindly people gone happily to the dogs.

21. No existing financial-accounting system actually measures an increase in true wealth; it measures an increase in the nominal increase of money-values, or, similarly, relative purchasing power. The latter often, as in the case of the U.S.A. since about March 1, 1968, involves an increase of nominal values in an economy which is in net physical decline, and is an implicitly doomed society, on precisely that account. The required physical measurement is, as opposed to the "I feel richer" delusion, an increase of the rate of increase of both the physical standard of living and its continuing, long-term accumulation of physical productivity per capita and per square kilometer of territory.

---

20. The reader must not overlook the crucially important scientific point which I have emphasized repeatedly, on earlier occasions. Species do not "compete" as individual species, but, dynamically, through the

The choice of pathway which actually leads toward survival, is, therefore, up to you. It is your choice as a citizen; your choice, of prosperity or doom. What is certain is, that life can not go on, on this planet, in the way we, as a planet, or Europe and the Americas, more narrowly, have gone in recent decades, especially since the dates of the famous assembly of the so-called "Warren Commission" and Rachel Carson's fraudulent, 1962 **Silent Spring**..

Although *the use of money* (rather than money itself) is an extremely important aspect of the organizing of the creative process on which a successful national, or world economy depends, it is sheer idiocy, as I have already emphasized here so far, to presume, as the unfortunately customary financial accountant does today, that the notion of value within the economic process is primarily a reflection of a monetary process, or to presume that financial growth is in itself either a cause of, or even a measure, even an approximate measure of real growth. The emphasis on financial accounting in the small, which is the legacy of the history of imperialism in general, and of, unfortunately, today's usually taught economics in particular, is the most common source of the most incompetent judgments in general accounting practice, and in the practice among professional economists in particular.

For example: the so-called "Robinson Crusoe" hypothesis, as by the Bertrand Russell devotees and science-quacks John von Neumann and Oskar Morgenstern,[22] is currently at the root of the clearest, and relatively most influential expression of the prevalent, wild forms of dogma influencing public policy-shaping in Europe and elsewhere throughout the world today.

The Science of Physical Economy

Insofar as there has been successful increase of both the physical standard of living and populations so far, these happier outcomes have depended upon both physical-scientific progress in human behavior, and a relative increase of both the physical standard of living of the population, as measured both per capita and per square kilometer, and as expressed in an increase of the relative physical rate of capital-intensity per capita and

per square kilometer of its habitation. Without those improvements, societies would necessarily degenerate in both physical standard of living per capita of the population as whole, and in the potential relative population density of territory inhabited by mankind. So, the economy of the U.S.A. has degenerated since the effect of the Warren Commission.[23]

Said otherwise, not only mankind's progress, but even its population as a whole, depends upon the realization of the effect of a combined science-driven and Classical-culture-driven increase in the population's *potential relative population-density.*

A competent science of physical economy depends upon the complementarity of two great principles. The first pertains to the processes within the Lithosphere and Biosphere; the second, ruling consideration, pertains to those human powers of individual creativity which are expressed immediately, and as if originally, in the domain of the singing of Classical poetry. It is in the latter domain that the immediacy of human individual creativity is to be recognized.

It is Classical science in, for example, the Platonic tradition, which generates the increase of a culture's potential relative population-density. It is Classical culture which promotes, in the individual mind and social process, as Percy Shelley emphasized in his **A Defence of Poetry**, the spark of creativity on which society's scientific creativity depends. It is the spirit of Johann Sebastian Bach's unique, original development in music, which enhances poetry to such heard effect, and illuminates the mind's power to recognize the eyes of the "Bust of Homer" as contemplating the contemptible spectacle of a virtually brain-dead, almost reptilian fop, Aristotle.

Take the case, for example, of the drawing down of existing sources of potable fresh water. The supplies are being drained by the existing population, even at the rates of consumption by the great masses of the world's terribly poor. Only a general increase in the energy-flux-density throughput could solve this problem, an increase which were not possible generally without reliance on rapid increases in the number of gigawatts of power uttered at the very high energy-flux density of

---

22. John von Neumann and Oskar Morgenstern, **Theory of Games and Economic Behavior**, 3rd edition (Princeton: Princeton University Press: 1953).

23. The point made by me here is aptly illustrated by the contrast of the effects of the Kennedy economic policy of avoiding the prospect of an unnecessary U.S. combat in Indo-China, with the ruinous effects of the policies launched under the influence behind the Warren Commission.

"Aristotle Contemplating a Bust of Homer," by Rembrandt van Rijn, 1753. Actually, LaRouche says, it is the power of the "blind" poet's mind that contemplates "the virtually brain-dead, almost reptilian fop, Aristotle."

modern nuclear-fission power-plants.

This is also the case for other essential mineral resources.[24]

Much of our planet's high-grade mineral resources are being drawn down similarly. Only very high energy-flux-density applications, by mankind, of physical chemistry, and of physical bio-chemistry, can conquer this trend. Only the mind of man can create those needed applications.

There are two leading consequences of such trends. First, as the history of overcoming this problem has already demonstrated, advances in technology which depend, in a critical way, upon both increases in physical-capital intensity per capita and per square kilometer, and successive breakthroughs to higher orders of scientific progress can bring such potential problems

under control *indefinitely*. The cases of nuclear-fission power, now, and thermonuclear fusion as a leading power-source, soon, illustrate the policy requirements for assured, continuing human upward survival.

An increasing ration of investment in high energy-flux-density modes in infrastructure, in addition to high energy-flux-density, and increasing capital-intensity of required patterns of investment in capital formation, must be combined with an immediate emphasis on capital-intensive modes in productivity of productive labor. This means greening of deserts, and a trend toward organized development of forests in areas which have been deserts during much of the recent nearly 20,000 "post-glacial" years.

This means, of course, an increase in scientific education which reverses the recent forty-five years trend against science-driven, capital-intensive progress in production and infrastructure, in the U.S.A. and other so-called "industrialized economies." It means, above all, an accelerating rate of increase of energy-flux density in quantities of power generated per capita and per square kilometer, and in modalities of generation of power for all general purposes.

This signifies, rather obviously, a change in policies of education, to emphasize a combined science-driver orientation to people today, but, also, a nonetheless essential return to emphasis on Classical artistic modes in education and cultural life generally.

Above all else, such as reversal of the present global, nearly five decades of drift, since the assassination of President John F. Kennedy, of today's increasingly decadent civilization's majority of populations toward an eagerly sought, early arrival at Hell, it is the ridding of populations of the grip of decadent popular cultures, such as ending the decadence of the so-called popular musical culture of the U.S.A.'s and Europe's recent four decades and longer, which must gain a leading place in our intentions.

Looking back over preceding millennia, to such times as those of the ancient Delphi cult and its Apollo-Dionysos depravities, a relevant study of this matter of comparative cultural histories and their respective ef-

---

24. Although the existence of large masses of water is itself a product of life.

The Baby Boomer generation and their children have been led by such would-be Pied Pipers as Al Gore, to "horrid destinations typified by the drug cultures of marijuana, opium, and cocaine."

fects, shows us that the popular basis for the presently accelerating dive of the entire planet toward Hell, expresses a modern echo of the ancient Dionysian cult, an impulse which has been chiefly driven through the influence exerted by the British Empire's psychological-warfare practices during the post-Franklin Roosevelt years of the planet at large. It has been only by stupefying the great majorities of the nations and their populations, especially those children of middle- and upper-class families born since the death of President Franklin Roosevelt, that mankind could have been self-induced, so widely, to seek to destroy itself by means of such moral and intellectual depravity as the popular anti-nuclear, anti-science culture of Britain's Prince Philip today.

It has been as if the manipulation of President Harry S Truman by the British Empire's Winston Churchill and the like, had lured the "68er" phenomenon exhibited among the children sired by our Baby Boomer generation, into the never-land to which some Pied Piper had misled them and the institutions of government which their "68er"-style moral and intellectual sicknesses pollute today.

What is destroying civilization now, is the substitution of pleasure in the popularity of perverse depravi-

ties through which that porcine would-be Pied Piper Al Gore would lead them, to horrid destinations typified by the drug cultures of marijuana, opium, and cocaine. They have rejected their own birthright, like the people of the fabled "Cities of the Plain," their rejection of the joy of making a contribution to the immortality and improvement of our human species while we are alive to do so. The British Empire has robbed the world in many ways, in genocide against Black Africa and other ways, but the worst of all its crimes are not so much physical, as they have been the intended destruction of the morality of its prey, including the populations of Europe and North America.

Herein, as I shall emphasize, lies the evidence of the essential root of the difference between a credit-system, as understood by great U.S. patriots such as Alexander Hamilton, and the monetary systems which are, in fact, the presently essential expression of imperialism.

Monetarism: A Currency, or a Disease?

I state flatly, without fear of the existence of any possibly competent objection, that *money does not express actual economic value*. Indeed, any effort to propose, or merely assume the notion of a monetary value, or a financial-accounting system as actually representing economic value, represents a blending of the intention inhering in more or less vicious types of the practice of the evil of usury.

The most evil form of expression of usury today, a practice which should be classed as intrinsically a crime against humanity, is typified by the British imperialist system associated with such names from the imperialist repertoire of the notorious paid prostitutes of the British East India Company's Lord Shelburne, as Adam Smith and Jeremy Bentham.

Imperialism is very old in known history. The relatively more recent among the known forms of imperialism are traced from the Mediterranean-centered imperialism of the Peloponnesian War, during which two rival imperialist parties, Sparta and Athens, fought out a brutal-like warfare for supremacy, warfare which ended, ultimately with the common ruin of ancient Greece, with the onrushing supremacy of what became the

Roman Empire, over the crushed remains of its former rivals.

All such imperial conflicts within known European history of maritime cultures, have been imperialist ventures premised upon the notion of the supremacy of a usurious form of the privately owned money-system of an imperial elite circle, as typified by the utter moral and practical degeneracy of British empiricist ideology since the ruin of its only real challenger, the U.S.A., through the developments from the post-August 1971 disruption of the sovereignty of the U.S. dollar through the establishment of the Anglo-Dutch-Saudi financier interests' dominant position in what became established as the hegemonic, petroleum spot-market system.

The only actually scientific standard of economic value, is not a monetary standard, but a human one: the indispensable, and endless increase of the potential relative productive powers of labor expressed per capita and per square kilometer of territory. This notion of value subsumes, as I have already noted, above, the need to do more than merely compensate for the depletion of what had been the preferred natural resources obtained from what the followers of Academician V.I. Vernadsky have identified as the Lithosphere and Biosphere.

Money is merely an important convenience for the conduct of transactions within the economy in the small; it is not necessarily a determinant of economic value, but an agency for determining the assigned relative monetary value within the bounds of a relatively fixed monetary system, as Alexander Hamilton defined Federal national banking, and as Franklin Roosevelt made the crucial contribution to making possible the defeat of the Nazi system which the British monarchy had brought into existence in continental Europe. No natural increase of wealth occurs through the free circulation of money as such. Wealth must be produced, essentially as either improved physical products, or the improvement of the powers of the individual human mind.

Today's world tends to deplete those accessible richer resources of the Lithosphere, and must act to enhance the richness of the Biosphere as such richness might be estimated in *per-capita* and *per-square-kilometer* terms. In general, on the first such account, our continued existence and progress as a species of a certain minimal potential population-density, depends upon those qualitative advances in scientific-techno-logical progress, per capita and per square kilometer, which are to be measured as both the advantage of fundamental, qualitative advances in applied science, and in a general increase of the ratio of investment in a potentially productive quality of development of the human environment, per capita, and in energy-flux-density of the modes of power employed.

This progress depends upon qualitative advances in both the intellectual powers and habits of the general population, per capita and per square kilometer, to which the modalities of that progress are applied in what is implicitly an increasingly physical-capital-intensive investment mode.

Since this excellent intention is expressed by the individual personalities of a society, it is necessary to make possible scientific and related progress in such matters, through the means of the way in which society's internal social processes are organized. The required modality of such organization is centered, essentially, on those creative mental powers of the individual which are the only true distinction of the human individual from the baboon, or baboon-like, usually very greedy human creatures of prominence in Wall or Threadneedle streets, or kindred places. Such naughty prominences include certain presently, politically high-ranking ones, whose names I shall refrain from listing in this presently immediate literary location, but whose names are either readily known, or readily accessible to many in the ranks of popular opinion today.

For this purpose, a successful mode of existence of a modern economy uses a form of money as credit, as a monopoly of a sovereign nation, not as an intrinsic form of functional economic value. This is properly done, as the U.S. Federal Constitution's law respecting both the fundamental principles of law set forth in its Preamble, prescribes implicitly, and as the specific U.S. Federal Constitutional provisions require respecting uttering of monetizable credit and enactment of treaty-agreements.

During the immediate post-World War II interval, the 1950s most notably, the idea of monetary valuation of purchase and sale of products, and of earned incomes, was based on a compromise associated with the phrase "fair trade." This was a notion which echoed a residue of the then-adult population's refreshed experience of the general economic growth and prosperity brought about through the Constitution-based initiatives of the general economic recovery from depression and Wall Street fascists' hegemonies, accomplished

The terrorizing of President Johnson by the assassination of President Kennedy (shown here in the motorcade in Dallas), and the Warren Commission's suppression of any honest investigation, facilitated radical changes in U.S. policy. Below, the Warren Commission presents its report to President Johnson, Sept. 24, 1964. Left to right: John J. McCloy, J. Lee Rankin (general counsel), Sen. Richard Russell, Rep. Gerald Ford, Chief Justice Earl Warren, President Johnson, former CIA director Allen Dulles, Sen. John Sherman Cooper, and Rep. Hale Boggs.

Lyndon B. Johnson Library/Cecil Stoughton

under the administration of President Franklin Roosevelt. This view persisted until the aftermath of the assassination of President John F. Kennedy, ostensibly done by British imperial interests, and their fellow-travellers, interests operating behind such instruments as the largely Ibero-American-based teams of highly trained assassins associated with the mass of efforts deployed in the attempt to assassinate France's President Charles de Gaulle.

The terrorizing of President Lyndon Johnson by both the Kennedy assassination itself, as President Johnson himself pointed toward that fact in a later time, and the Anglo-American Tory faction of the Wall Street crowd's rapidly installed suppression, by the Warren Commission, of any honest investigation, facilitated the radical changes in policy and adopted destiny of the U.S.A., and of nations such as France, Germany, and Italy, in the ensuing years of that decade. I know this

very well, since I came to recognize the same problem dominating many facets of my own personal and general political environment during the 1960s, 1970s, and also in the matter of the SDI, and still, in comparable ways, today.

Those political influentials who condoned Enron, or the monstrous swindle of the people of the U.S.A. by the continuing bail-out of Wall Street bandits such as the circles of Presidential advisor Larry Summers and his frankly fellow-fascist, Behavioralist gang of lunatics today, represent a kind of infection with moral diseases which are now threatening to carry the United States and its people down to the Hell which a grandly larcenous Larry Summers appears to have chosen for his own ultimate destiny, pending his arrival to what is ostensibly his compulsive groping for eternal infamy.[25]

---

25. The popular wit around observers of the Obama administration, is, that when Peter Orszag removes his toupee, the head comes off, sooner or later. The sooner President Obama chucks that pack of fascistic clowns, Larry Summers and Summers' behaviorist accomplices down the political waste-chute, with their Hitler-copied schemes for mass euthanasia in the misused name of health-care, the sooner the President himself would cease his recent flirtation with infamy, and might become honorably successful, instead.

II. Whence Our Credit-System Came

There are only two strategically crucial, respectively distinct species of economic systems available to our planet today. The oldest of those two, presently existing systems, is *the imperialist system*, otherwise known more popularly today as *a monetarist system,* which is the modern form of monetarism modeled today on the teachings of both the followers of the imperialists Adam Smith and Jeremy Bentham,[26] and of the pro-fascist, John Maynard Keynes.[27] The only presently significant, existing alternative to that intrinsically imperialist system, is the original Constitutional system of the United States of America, which is based on what is known otherwise as *an explicitly anti-Anglo-Dutch, Hamiltonian credit system of national banking.*

The option now available to the citizens of the U.S.A., among others, is: either we choose a return to Hamilton's principle of national banking, or accept the accelerating, mass-murderous increase in the death-rate proposed by President Obama's implicitly Hitler-copied, "useless eaters" dogma of such as Larry Summers and Peter Orszag.. This should be a warning not only to the citizens of the U.S.A., but every nation of the world which really cares about the survival of its own people. Do not wait, as many German victims of Nazism did, until it is to late to stop the likes of Orszag today.

---

26. Adam Smith and Jeremy Bentham were the British East India Company's officially adopted authors of the present, frankly fascist program of both President Obama's advisors Larry Summers and the Behaviorist circles of the certifiably, frankly fascist 1968er Peter Orszag, et al. See Adam Smith, **Theory of Moral Sentiments** (1759) and Jeremy Bentham's **An Introduction to the Principles of Morals and Legislation** (1780). From 1782 on, Bentham was Lord Shelburne's principal agent for the special operations of the newly created British Foreign Office, and the predecessor and patron of the Lord Palmerston who owned, among others, the Foreign Office's unwitting asset and Palmerston agent, Giuseppe Mazzini's Karl Marx. Marx was also, for a time, supervised for the British Foreign Office by veteran British diplomat and recording secretary of Mazzini's Young Europe, David Urquhart. British spy Alexander Helphand ("Parvus") was a later element of this British intelligence operation, an operation which overlapped British weapons-trafficking and the same British channels controlling the "Young Turks" who organized the massacre of an estimated one million Armenians under their reign.

27. See Keynes' own introduction to his original 1987 (German) edition of his General System, in which he states his preference for the economic-social system of Adolf Hitler's Germany over that of other nations. On the significance of Keynes' systematically fascist roots, see below.

I also emphasize: Either the world now adopts an explicitly Hamiltonian form of credit-system, or, therefore, the world is presently, already plunging toward a chasm of global genocide engulfing all peoples of the world, that at a presently accelerating rate. This means a collapse from which the specific, presently existing political systems of the planet could never recover a semblance of their present form. There are no local options available to any nation, which might exempt it from that rule; there is no possible recovery of any nation, except through the present introduction of that great, global reform represented by a turn to what I shall describe here as a "Hamiltonian" solution, as the remedy for the cancer of Keynesian or kindred monetarism.

I am not stating that Hamilton's design was the one-and-only path to paradise. I mean that the global situation created by the system of financial derivatives which was allowed by the reign of Federal Reserve Chairman Alan Greenspan inside the U.S.A. itself, has produced a presently global, general breakdown-crisis of such a nature than no other remedy than Hamilton's could avert a presently onrushing, imminently hyper-inflationary breakdown-crisis of the entire planetary system. For certain special reasons, which I shall indicate in due course, here, the only present hope for the planet as a whole, is an initiative to this effect by the Federal government, especially by the institution of the Presidency of these United States, even despite the present incumbent's, presently, thoroughly incompetent, and worse, policies.

Therefore, the message to all the nations of the world is, that either the President of the U.S.A., presently Barack Obama, accepts the policy which I have just identified, or it might be fair to say, that the entire planet is now on its way to what would seem to be a state of Hell beyond the belief of most living today.

Therefore, in the interest of setting the stage of history for presenting the case for a global credit-system, a system to replace the otherwise hopelessly bankrupt, present world monetary system, we should do as I prescribe here: consider the following observations on the matter of the role of the virtual treason implicit in the presently experienced ruin of the economy of our United States, a ruin which began, as if on the night before syphilis, through the actions of President Harry S Truman beginning April 13, 1945, the day after the death of President Franklin Roosevelt.

As a consequence of the virtually treasonous subversion of the U.S.A. by that impassioned sympathizer of Winston Churchill's imperial London, President Harry S Truman,[28] my republic abandoned the true sovereignty of that American System of political-economy which had been the leader among nations. In this way, our republic abandoned the dedication of President Franklin D. Roosevelt to our role as the world's leader in the anti-colonialist cause of the benefit of the peoples of the nations at large. Our U.S. economy was to be, ultimately, ruined, even to the degree that we are experiencing that now. The further result of that ruin, which was planted then like a British seed, by Truman, has become, today, the massive, spiraling, implicitly treasonous reign of ruin which we of the U.S.A. have been experiencing since the close of August, 2007.

Specifically, that assortment of pro-Mussolini and pro-Adolf Hitler crowds running loose among us, during the 1920s and 1930s, especially Wall Street types, had been the outgrowth of what had been already the form of London's traditional set of British agents lodged within the U.S.A. since the early Eighteenth Century. These are, still today, in the main, the collective descendants of the British East India Company's American agents, known today as that "Wall Street" crowd which is a true replica of what the Roosevelt time's Pecora commission would regard as the larcenous Goldman Sachs, et al. of today. That is the crowd which had lately undermined our American system more, and more boldly: especially since that turn in world history which has been continued since the successfully attempted, November 22, 1963, assassination of President John F. Kennedy.

Subsequently, through the implicitly treasonous actions to the same effect, we have what was provided, largely, by the proverbial "rats in the ship's hold" of our ship of state. These were the types which the Dionysian cult's tradition formed as the so-called "68ers," was composed. As a result of that 1968 turn, the accumulated intellectual and economic capital stock of the U.S.A. has been wrecked by the combination of not only such witting and impassioned agents of Dionysian evil as those, but also through the complicity shown by their cowardly accomplices drawn into the games played among many of the leading Baby Boomers in

our political system, such as House Speaker Nancy "Off the Table" Pelosi, today.[29]

That downward trend in the economies of both the U.S.A. and the world economy taken as a whole, was continued in what has been an implicitly treasonous fashion, by such agencies as David Rockefeller's Trilateral Commission. Following the Trilateral Commission's initial, 1977-1981 reign of ruin, the world economy, when considered as that single whole which it has virtually become today, was already being virtually destroyed, over the course of the 1980s, destroyed through the complicity of the role which President George H. W. Bush would play in backing the British rape of Europe by the initiatives of Britain's Fabian-style Tory, Prime Minister Margaret Thatcher, and her principal European continental accomplice, France's President François Mitterrand.[30]

That post-1989 destruction of western and central continental Europe, chiefly by London, done through that looting of post-1989 Germany and also of the Soviet Union's formerly associated Comecon states of eastern Europe, has now been extended in the form of the presently continuing waves of strategically crucial looting which London had unleashed, back then, unleashed, with President George H.W. Bush's complicity, against what had been both the peoples and territory of the Soviet Union and its former Comecon associates. This process of looting is being continued by London and its accomplices up through the present day.

For most of those leading victims of London and its lackeys who have been turned loose upon the political circles in western and central Europe today, submission to London is expressed as implicitly, "our own ruin is our natural European destiny!"

The net physical output of all Europe, in particular,

<hr>

28. If, and when we acknowledge the actual principle on which the American constitutional system of government depends, as admittedly few relevant academic pedagogues and justices of today do, the insertion of a British notion of liberalism as the premise of economic policy, is, in and of itself, a treasonous impulse.

29. Observers who did not think with clear heads, alleged the "68ers" to be socialists—"the left." To those of us who knew better, the term socialist had signified, earlier, concern for the physical improvement and freedom of the generality of the population, and also the benefits of scientific and technological progress of the nation. Whatever the aberrations of notable socialist groups had been, that was clear. The 68ers came on the stage of history, hating farmers and "blue collar" labor, and committed to destroying the scientific and technological progress on which progress in the conditions of life of ordinary folk depend. The 68ers were, like the circles of Mark Rudd, therefore, essentially fascists, as this has been their continued legacy, from that time, to the present day.

30. The sympathies for Hitler's Nazis by the father of de-facto British agent George H.W. Bush, and George H.W. Bush's close ties to the British monarchy have been highly relevant elements of the corruption which led to the top-down betrayal of republic's constitutional order.

per capita and per square kilometer of territory, has been collapsed, catastrophically, falling to levels there far below those of 1989.

Elsewhere from around the world, even what had been the expansion of China's export economy, during the post-1989 interval, has now experienced a recent, deep-cutting reversal of its earlier trend of growth. This had been a growth which reflected the use, by the U.S.A. and western Europe, especially, of expanded cheap-labor markets of the world as a means for collapsing what had been previously the best developed physical economies of the world as a whole. That has now been changed, abruptly, and radically.

Now, China's well-being is threatened by its dependency on those foreign markets for its exports, markets which have now virtually ceased to exist. Now, since the critical point reached in late July through August, 2007, the world as a whole has been plunged into an accelerating collapse of its already, hopelessly, financially bankrupted physical economy. Now, the policies adopted earlier, if continued today, represent an onrushing ruin from which no economic recovery of either China, or any other nation, would ever occur in the life-times of all those living today.

This would be the result in fact, if the continuation of the presently reigning financial-monetary systems, such as the present form of the so-called European system, were still allowed. The world as a whole is already sliding over the steepening, crumbling brink, toward the deep, Hellish chasm of doom, a doom lying, seemingly, inches beyond every next tick of the global clock today.

It is not difficult to show, by valid evidence available to any economically literate, intelligent, and also sane person, that all monetary systems tend, by their nature, to be instruments of an imperial form of international monetary power. All monetary systems operating within an established climate of so-called "free trade," are expressions of imperialist systems of outright tyranny, systems operating on behalf of a specific set of those financier interests which have succeeded in placing themselves now, as, intrinsically, in a form of imperial reign over the world as a whole.

Actually, on calm reflection, we must admit that this has been the role of a system over which the outgrowth of maritime expressions of the outgrowths of what had been the ancient Mediterranean maritime form of monetary system, now rule. These predators have tended to rule, always in some similar fashion, since such precedents as the heyday of that ancient Tyre pulled down by Alexander the Great, or, the later emergence, with aid of the Mithra-cult representatives stationed on the notorious Isle of Capri, of the Roman Empire under Augustus Caesar.

It is those kinds of echoes of this past, which have provided, still, up to the present moment, the motives for the current pattern of self-inflicted onrush of doom now menacing the world's civilization as a whole. This is a pattern which must be explored now in a way freed of consoling delusions. Such problems reflect the essential difference between the course of animal life, and the long-wave characteristics of both the social diseases, and also the remedies, which remain specific to mankind alone.

To understand that crucial distinction of the history of mankind from the records of animal life, we should proceed here from informed views of what had been such precedents for the present situation, as the imperial essence of the Roman and Byzantine empires seen at the breaking-points which had come the peak of their respective powers earlier. Since the decline of Byzantium, which became evident beginning approximately A.D. 1000, the hegemonic power ruling from above the world's emerging nations lying beneath, has been an association of monetarist interests centered in Venice, except for those pre-1968-1973 intervals when our U.S.A.'s constitutional credit-system was not only willing, but enabled, as under Presidents Abraham Lincoln and Franklin Delano Roosevelt, to hold the nominally British imperial tyranny in check.

That Empire Itself

The present world empire is what has been called the British Empire; apart from the virtually childish fantasies of some, there is, in fact, no other empire presently existing on this planet. However, that empire, loosely described as British, is still, implicitly, a continued extension of its historical root in the imperial role of a medieval and modern Venice which surpassed the financial-monetary power of its former mother, Byzantium, since about A.D. 1000. That rise of Venetian maritime-monetary power had occurred, notably, long after the death of Charlemagne had eliminated the only earlier, real challenger, his France, to the imperial power of Byzantium. The rise of Venice to implicitly imperial power at declining Byzantium's expense, came at the time when Venice had moved into a dominant role as a center of organized international monetarist power, as in the time of Venice's role in the orchestration of the so-called "Crusades;" the now. slime-mold-like, Venetian monetarist oligarchy, has, essentially, retained that ill-concealed kind of its imperial monetary power, still, to the present day.[31]

Unfortunately, that use of the term "British Empire," while fairly said, resonates with the usual effect of misleading the more poorly educated hearers; what reigns today, is still essentially the Venetian oligarchical system of monetarism; but, now, since the rise of the influence of Paolo Sarpi, with the Liberal (and also frequently fascist) system of a Venetian interest operating under a now Sarpian Liberal form, the notion of a "British" or "Anglo-Dutch Liberal" empire is the qualified, popular brand-label for the presently adopted expression of a Venetian monetarists' imperial system. The City of London is, for the moment, the place where the public offices of that traditionally Venetian monetarist empire, are still ostensibly located, as if for no better excuse than the convenience of the economic illiterates who might lack knowledge of the global system's actually proper, Venetian, home address.

The spirit of Venice, speaking as if with the voice of a deadly disease, says to the British Empire, "In the end, we, the heirs of the true, still-living Roman empire, own you!" Such is the essence of the underlying social composition of monetarism.

That part played by Britain, is the key to understanding what might be, for many stubbornly befuddled citizens, still, the otherwise obscured, actual role of the present U.S. Obama Presidency.

We must take into account, but not exaggerate that Presidency's power. At most recent report, President Obama is still a virtual puppet of international financier interests. He bears a London label pinned, by Her Majesty, onto his made-in-Wall Street political attire, but, his office remains, for the moment, a product of a Venetian imperial monetarist interest, that all the way down to the essential roots of its British, e.g., "brutish," behaviorist threads of its soul. So, the current welfare, pension, and health schemes pushed by the frankly-as-fascist-as-Hitler gang identified by Larry Summers and the Behaviorist psychologists, such as the, fortunately, still intrinsically politically expendable Peter Orszag.

"Globalization," otherwise nicknamed "free trade," is to be recognized as an "empire writ large," an empire to be recognized as "Globalization's" now proposed, immediate successor to what is becoming, rapidly, our ruined United States, a former U.S.A. being digested now by the intestines of that imperial power which is being assigned, by current intention, to become a proposed (sic!) new, global, Tower of "Babble."

Of course, were President Obama freed from his administration's presently assigned "Uncle Tom" status as an obedient kisser of the butt of London, his government might be found, by London and Venice, as changed into being a very troublesome fellow for those London monetarists' attempts to continue to manage him. However, unfortunately, for the present moment, as I write those lines, the costume which he is currently wearing, is, still, the trappings of his present, puppet-like servitude, a costume which he wears, for a little while, somewhat like dictator Mussolini, with evident, comi-tragically Caesarian pride.

Somewhere, the deceased Winston Churchill, who once owned Benito Mussolini, is giggling from his grave about that.

Alexander Hamilton's Remedy

That much now said to situate the case immediately at hand, we have come now to the time to consider the following.

The true economic and related authority of the United States of America among nations generally, has always resided, for longer than that republic has existed, in an impulse first expressed, approximately, in the pre-1688-89 internal economic organization of my relevant ancestors' Massachusetts Bay Colony of that time, as also implicit in the Mayflower Compact.

This early, New Englanders' commitment, still expresses its deep roots in European history. For example: a glance at the true story of the first successful transAtlantic voyage by Christopher Columbus, is crucial for understanding how our United States came into being, nearly three centuries later. That part of the personal history of Columbus began for him, about A.D. 1480, when Columbus had learned of the last great discovery of the great Cardinal Nicholas of Cusa, through access, in Portugal, to documents authored by Cusa

---

31. Venetian imperialism, still today, is expressed in the guise of a collective set of oligarchical family interests crafted, explicitly, according to the ancient Roman imperial precedents. Such formations must be examined dynamically, rather than as in a Cartesian image of loose parts. The families are "members of the club," such that the list of the names of the members may be altered, but it is the club as such which reigns in its constitution as a conspiratorial oligarchy of families. Anyone who denies the role of such conspiracies, is either a liar or virtually a babbling idiot.

during the last part of Cusa's life.

As Columbus had learned, the mission which Cusa had defined for the future of modern European civilization, had come to Cusa as a reflection on a worsening trend in European civilization since the role of the Venetians in bringing about the Fall of a Constantinople which was already no more than a vestigial political power, but still a culturally crucial one, as its part in the great ecumenical Council of Florence had already demonstrated, conclusively, during the preceding decades.

Cusa had concluded, that under those culturally perilous circumstances, the mission of modern European civilization required its launching of expeditions crossing oceans, to establish ties in places found thus. It was the documents, by Cusa himself, as part of his legacy, which came before the eyes of a Genoese sea-captain in the service of Portugal, Christopher Columbus. From about A.D. 1480, Columbus was personally committed to cross the Atlantic to make contact with the people residing on the other shores of the Atlantic. He was enabled to accomplish that inspired mission in A.D. 1492 at about the distance expected on the map he used, reaching that goal during the beginning of the time of the onset of the terrible developments, a spread of what was to become Europe-wide religious warfare, beginning that same year. This was the warfare launched by those Venice-steered, Habsburg imperialists who were deeply dedicated to the attempted ruin of the legacy of both Nicholas of Cusa and of that great ecumenical Council of Florence which had been assembled for its great civilizing mission, which had occurred in the place where the completion of the cupola of Santa Maria del Fiore, was being celebrated at that time.

As a consequence of these developments associated with Nicholas of Cusa and his great civilizing legacy, Columbus' evangelical mission, coming, thus, at a time of the collapse of Europe into the prolonged religious warfare of A.D. 1492-1648, was to inspire waves of courageous colonization, launched from a war-tormented Europe, into the hopeful chances which might be sought across the Atlantic. What was to prove to be the most crucial of these changes came in A.D. 1620, in the area known as Massachusetts.

From our present vantage-point, the historical significance of those trans-Atlantic voyagers has been typified most efficiently by the two settlements in Seventeenth Century New England, by the A.D.1620 Mayflower Compact and the subsequent, A.D. 1635 establishment of the Massachusetts of the Winthrops and Mathers. These settlers were no refugees, but theirs were the efforts of pioneers dedicated to enshrine the best of the cultural achievements of modern European civilization at a relative distance from the system of oligarchical reigns and warfare then dominating a post-Renaissance Europe, that to an often greatly discouraging degree since, still today.

The mission of such voyagers as those was to preserve the best of modern European culture in a form freed of the oligarchical depravity sitting in Europe, even still today, on top of, and in opposition to that great legacy of that Fifteenth-century Renaissance typified by both the friends of Nicholas of Cusa and by the initiation of such true modern, sovereign nation-states carrying forward such Renaissance principles of civilization, as expressed by Louis XI's France and Louis' admirer, Henry VII of England.

This is of critical importance, for the sake of today's urgent need for a deeper understanding of the unique virtues of the Federal Constitution of the United States. It must be recognized that the founders of the relevant leading English-speaking (and also a considerable number of German-speaking[32]) colonists which composed what was to become the Federal government of the United States, came to our shores not as refugees, but as those whose intentions were to be founders of a composition of society conceived in the intentions inherited, in point of fact, from one of the greatest leaders in the founding of modern European civilization, Cardinal Nicholas of Cusa, and, later, during the Eighteenth Century, the influence of Gottfried Leibniz.

I repeat this emphasis on volunteers, rather than refugees, as my point here, because my emphasis is not only truthful, but is of crucial historical importance for understanding the cultural roots of, and, thus, the roots of the cure for the presently threatened, worldwide economic breakdown-crisis of the present moment.[33]

On that account, to make clear the mandatory reform on whose model the world as a whole now depends for our escape from a presently onrushing descent into global barbarism, I must repeat myself here, in order to situate and amplify a point which I introduced at the outset of this report. Without taking these matters into account in the fashion I now treat them here, there could

---

32. Especially into Pennsylvania.
33. I intend to imply the allusion here, to the principle of dynamics, as emphasized by Percy Bysshe Shelley in the concluding paragraph of his **A Defence of Poetry**.

The drafting of the Declaration of Independence in Philadelphia, 1776. Left to right: Benjamin Franklin, the political and cultural heir of the Winthrops and the Mathers; John Adams; and Thomas Jefferson.

Europe. In Europe, freedom tended to arrive belatedly, following the explosion of horrors expressed by the French Revolution and Napoleon Bonaparte's emulation of the folly of the earlier "Seven Years War." Within Europe itself, Europe's spurts of struggle for true freedom came usually as a kind of difficult compromise with the oligarchical powers, a compromise which Europe's and other parliamentary systems reflect, still today.

On this point, if we examine the pre-1688 Massachusetts, before the British monarchy's military exertions temporarily crushed the independence of that colony, we see what later proved to be the seeds planted in the republican spirit of the original colonists, seeds expressed in the forms of self-government and development there, including the roots of what would be, later, the eruption of a credit system, rather than a monetary system of the type which is still an habitual inclination in most of Europe today.

Our Declaration of Independence and Federal Constitution, are the most crucial among the important consequences of that missionary dedication of those parties of the European colonists who settled in North, Central, and South America. Such are the deeply rooted, special bonds which unite those among us in these Americas who have understood the special place in history which is shared among the true patriots of our Americas. Such was the specific inspiration of the original colonists led by the Winthrops and Mathers, by their political and cultural heir Benjamin Franklin, and embedded in the creation of the Declaration of Independence, Federal Constitution, and in the unique role of Alexander Hamilton's definition of a constitutional principle for an American System of political-economy. I speak of a principle, uttered by Hamilton, which is, still, in today's terribly menaced world as a whole, the only handy remedy for the gravest crisis overtaking all mankind in the perilous circumstances of this present moment of world history.

The Perils Now Before Us

What has come to be considered informed notions of law, even among some relatively decent officials in our own republic recently, has had, recently, only scant and increasingly rare relevance to the core body of natural law respecting the Preamble of our Federal Consti-

be no efficient comprehension of both the nature, and the urgent necessity, of the mandatory general economic reform which I place before you here today.

The principal issue expressed by the migration into those English colonies in North America, from which the core of our movement for independence sprang, was disgust, even hatred of the role, traditions, and habits associated with the dominant place of Europe's oligarchical strata of that time. Such was the hatred of oligarchy expressed by the more spirited souls from among the language cultures of Europe.

That fact and its legacy are expressed most clearly, still today, in the instinctive preference of the Americans for a true republic, as opposed to a parliamentary form of government more typical of today's still presently embedded oligarchical cultural traditions of

tution. The systemically anti-Locke Preamble, which was conceived and inspired by Gottfried Leibniz's attack on the bestiality of Locke and his policies, reflected a quality of inspiration which was already the core principle of the 1776 Declaration of Independence, a principle which was affirmed, with broader and deeper implications, in the core of the U.S. Federal Constitution, its anti-Locke Preamble.[34]

This has been a principle which the British and their lackeys, the Spanish slave-traffickers, and also the unreconstructed former slave-holders of the world today, still prefer had never existed. This political difference, then, between the oligarchical forces of Europe and the opposing American republics, was expressed most clearly in the adoption of Hamilton's anti-monetarist principle of a credit system, a credit-system which is the core-principle of the design of our Federal Constitution, that according to Alexander Hamilton's initiative, and in opposition to that oligarchical legacy in law which is the root of a European monetary system, in general, still today. Here lie the deeper roots of the difference between an American credit-system, and a typical susceptibility for such folly among Europeans as what is, for them today, a "traditional" monetary system such as that of Keynes.

Cusa & the Westphalian Principle

However, at this point, I must emphasize once more, that the deeper roots of the American System of political economy, are to be found, still today, in that great Fifteenth Century Renaissance which is centered, still, in processes including the model influence radiated from the great work of Dante Alighieri; from the later, actual historical role of Jeanne d'Arc; and, from the deep-rooted traces of Charlemagne's great reforms

much earlier than either of those. Those were the roots, from which a new quality of institution was later to be assembled in the seminal work of such as Nicholas of Cusa, which is to be examined in the context of its crucial, contributing role in shaping the great ecumenical Council of Florence. The foundations of that modern, ecumenical principle of nation-state republic, which was affirmed by the 1648 Peace of Westphalia, and by the closely related founding of the institutions of modern physical science and economy, are to be recognized in the implications of those historical connections to Cusa's work for the entire world today.

It was against that same Fifteenth Century revolution in culture associated with, and expressed by the pivotal great ecumenical Council of Florence, that the Venetian financier oligarchy, which had already absorbed the subverted, putatively rival Genoa into its fold, acted in its promotion of the night-time opening of the gates of Constantinople to the Ottomans, that by the assigned guards, in A.D. 1453, and that event's role in the promotion of the later explosion of religious warfare of the A.D. 1492-1648 interval.

As I have said repeatedly in earlier locations, as also in earlier portions of this present writing, the transformation of a civilization which had been virtually destroyed, into becoming a system of modern sovereign nation-states, had been awakened and informed, that to a crucial degree of importance, by three leading, politically relevant writings of Nicholas of Cusa: 1.) His **Concordancia Catholica**, which contributed crucially to establishing the essential principle of the modern sovereign form of nation-state; 2.) His **De Docta Ignorantia**, which founded modern European science; and, 3.) his **De Pace Fidei**, which provided the precedent realized in the role of Cardinal Mazarin and others in the crafting of that 1648 Peace of Westphalia on which all civilized forms of modern statecraft and law depend absolutely today. That is a principle which should be, and must be now established as a fundamental principle of natural law of nations for such properly anti-imperialist institutions as what President Franklin Roosevelt had intended should become a destroyer of all colonial systems of the world, a United Nations Organization (UNO). Without adherence to such a principle, a UNO were a travesty crafted in the cynic's mere name of peace, rather than a morally competent body in the conduct of international law among the members of a world-wide system of perfectly sovereign republics.

The entire foundation of what became modern Eu-

---

34. E.g., Gottfried Leibniz, **New Essays on Human Understanding**. This work, Leibniz's second thorough attack on John Locke, composed in 1704, but withheld for reason of Leibniz's learning of Locke's death, was transmitted to Benjamin Franklin before its general publication, by the circles of Göttingen's Professor Abraham Kästner. This was the work which inspired the crucial features of law in the 1776 U.S. Declaration of Independence, and was also expressed in that underlying affirmation of Leibniz's natural law in the Preamble of the U.S. Federal Constitution. Franklin was later the personal guest of Kästner at Göttingen. Kästner was Germany's leading mathematician of the middle to late Eighteenth Century, one of the two principal teachers of Carl F. Gauss, and the sponsor of the playwright Gotthold Lessing of the Lessing-Moses Mendelssohn collaboration. Kästner was thus, in this and other roles, at the center of the late Eighteenth-century artistic and cultural renaissance in Europe.

ropean science, had been built up out of a resurrection of the ruined great scientific and other cultural legacies of the ancient Classical past, as the foundations of modern science were built up through the central, successive roles of Brunelleschi and Nicholas of Cusa. It was the immediate followers of Cusa, in science, such as Luca Pacioli, Leonardo da Vinci, and their outstanding follower, Johannes Kepler, on which all the notable essentials specific to modern science were based.

Those were the immediate historical foundations of such advances as occurred during the course of the Sixteenth Century and early decades of the Seventeenth. This legacy of the Fifteenth and Sixteenth centuries was crucial, but that fact is not sufficient for actually understanding the new wave of creative leadership which emerged around the organizing for, and establishment of the great 1648 Peace of Westphalia, a treaty upon which all of the truly great institutions of European culture, including that of the Americas, have depended up to the present moment. It is that Peace of Westphalia, whose adherence marks the distinction of the honorable from the Satanic, that in all globally extended European political and moral culture today. The connection between the crucial advances of the Fifteenth and Seventeenth centuries, respectively, such as the Council of Florence and the Peace of Westphalia, had been located most simply and immediately in the history of modern physical science, as in work of Brunelleschi and Cusa, earlier; these spirits typify those who provided the foundations for that mid-Seventeenth-Century, upward leap in what is to be recognized today, more immediately, in the competent practice of modern physical science as by Gottfried Leibniz, and the foundations of modern Classical music located in the outcome of the subsequent, Eighteenth-century, work of that great genius, Johann Sebastian Bach.

However, there is another distinction of crucial importance for today.

Cusa had also contributed another policy which, as I have noted, earlier, was crucial for the subsequent coming into being of our United States. In the aftermath of the Fall of Constantinople, and its ensuing developments, he had recognized the deeper implications of the fact, that ruling European, pro-oligarchical cultural traditions menaced the intentions of that great ecumenical Council of Florence on which the existence of a modern, post-feudal tradition in Europe depended.

This attack on civilization by what became the doctrine of the British empire, and also of the morally depraved former Prime Minister Tony Blair, as with Lord Shelburne, and, earlier, imperial Britain's adored image of the Roman Emperor Julian the Apostate, was an attack on Cusa's **De Pace Fidei**, an attack on the argument by Cusa on which the concept of the 1648 Peace of Westphalia was subsequently premised in the initiative of the great Papal peace-maker, Cardinal Jules Mazarin. That was the Peace of Westphalia which the thoroughly depraved British Prime Minister Tony Blair sought to destroy in an infamous Chicago address.

It Was Born in Boston

In principle, the American System of political-economy had been born in Boston, Massachusetts, as a system of scrip created by the government of the colony, a system of scrip used to promote public and private improvements, which had been introduced at a time that Massachusetts' economy was technologically, for a time, in advance of Britain in the matter of the spirit of manufactures, as the case of the Saugus Iron Works has often been referenced, since, as an illustration of this point. That bountiful use of scrip created by the authority of the government of Massachusetts, had been uprooted by the actions of the English monarchy of the tumultuous passage of power from James II to William and Mary. Nonetheless, the principle was maintained in the memory of Benjamin Franklin and others, as a legacy of the Winthrops and Mathers. It persisted, almost as a matter of instinct among such leading American patriots of the Eighteenth Century as the followers of Cotton Mather's injunctions, that great, Massachusetts-born, American genius Benjamin Franklin, most notably.

The precedent of scrip was revived at the prompting of another young American genius and an associate of the aging Franklin at that time, the Alexander Hamilton who had served as General and President George Washington's aide, and was to become, later, U.S. Secretary of the Treasury. It was that Hamilton, so situated, who created the principle of design for the American System of political-economy. Hamilton's conception of a sovereign system of national credit, is to be recognized, still today, as an echo of the same spirit which had launched the role of scrip during a notable period of the life of the Massachusetts Bay Colony. That system which Hamilton's authorship built, thus, into the foundations of the U.S. Federal Constitution, became the act of genius on which the rise to world-leading physical-economic power of our United States depended.

No presumed American, or other economist can be considered as actually competent in such matters, who has not yet learned, or begun to have learned, and also adopted, that lesson as virtually the essence of the American citizen's oath of allegiance to our United States. The great struggle for the existence and survival of our United States, against our constitutional republic's most persistent adversary, the British Empire, has been once won, and won again, periodically, repeatedly, as under President Abraham Lincoln, during our republic's past history, through a resort to that great principle of the use of the principle of a credit-system, that done in opposition to that great, perpetual adversary of our republic, which is the imperial monetary system typified by that British empire, which was founded in February 1763, under the leadership of Lord Shelburne's British East India Company.

That is the key to understanding the historic implications of the genius of President Franklin Roosevelt's rescue of a virtually bankrupted United States from the wreckage caused by less-than-patriotic Presidents such as Theodore Roosevelt, Woodrow Wilson, and Calvin Coolidge, or, the similar Presidents, later, Richard Nixon, and the eternally, and infernally notorious Bushes. This turns our attention to that outright traitor, the Vice-President Aaron Burr who, in turn, often appears to be the role-model, today, for that ever-slimy, greasy, smelly, whining and lying, somewhat Tennessee possum-like London lackey, and former Vice-President, Al "Sixteen-tons-and- the-Company-Store" Gore.

It is only a fully conscious, deliberate return to that great principle of economy which Hamilton's discovery and its influence embedded in our constitutional, great American System of political-economy, which could now rescue the planet as a whole from the presently accelerating plunge into a global new dark age of several generations' duration. This special destiny of our United States is lodged within the organic history of this hemisphere since those discoveries by Christopher Columbus which had been prompted by the person of one of the most gifted geniuses of modern European history, Cardinal Nicholas of Cusa.

To realize what a presently aching world now needs the most, we must now declare an existing state of general bankruptcy of the present international monetary system, and must, at the same time, declare our commitment to support those reforms by other sovereigns who seek, appropriately, to remedy their comparable afflictions by joining with us in use of comparable means for establishing a global system based on commitment to security for the sovereign credit of cooperating sovereign nations, nations who cooperate without compromising any of the essential, perfect sovereignties of cooperating other nations.

The task is comparable, in principle, if much broader and deeper in implications, to the reform of the U.S. banking system which was organized by President Franklin Roosevelt. This is said here in recognition of the most pertinent reality, that the vital interests of both Russia and the principal nations of Asia, could not be defended under present global conditions and trends, except by means of the specific type of anti-monetarist reform—i.e., anti-imperialist reform—which I indicate here. The alliance of those nations of Eurasia with the U.S.A., on this account, would constitute an overwhelming power for the cause of a reform which would have the unique advantage of its appeal of being in the presently urgent, common interest of each part of all mankind.

III. The New World System

At this juncture in the report, I must repeat, that all those presumed economists and leading political figures of the world's nations today, who utter statements presuming that there is the prospect of a recovery of all, or any part of the present world financial system, deserve to be awarded the quality of mental health protection awarded to those who scream "no fire" in already burning, crowded theaters; like deserters in warfare, by their hysterical denial of reality, they are endangering the lives of a great part of all civilization now.

Contrary to some widely expressed, wishful thinking from various quarters of this planet, there never will be, because there never could be, an actual recovery of this present world financial system, at any time, ever. Therefore, any official of any leading government who reports his, or her opinion that a recovery of this particular system is possible, is now to be regarded as a danger to the health and welfare of society.

Only a radically new world system could prevent the planet's plunge into a new dark age of this planet. Only under the condition that the President discharges the frankly fascist team of the so-called "behavioral psychologists" and their Nazi-designed present health-care and social-security schemes, could the administration of President Barack Obama be saved from going down with our ship of state. Under that condition, as I have said repeatedly, I am committed to using my rather unique competence, for saving that administration, if President Obama is willing.

The crucial issue for all mankind is: unless the entire planetary economic system is put, very soon, into a certain kind of general reorganization in bankruptcy, a change from a monetary system to a Hamiltonian credit system, the world as a whole would surely fall, soon, into a prolonged new dark age for humanity, with a consequently likely, and relatively rapid collapse of the world population to that goal of less-than-two-billions persons demanded by the "environmentalist" hoax of World Wildlife Fund representative Prince Philip.

To block the mass-murderous scheme of that Prince Philip, the term, urgently needed reform, means:

a.) cancelling the existence of the Liberal form of the present world monetary system, together with that monetary-system's own present, specific, integral treaty-agreements,

b.) if we intend the U.S.A., in particular, to survive the present crisis, we shall be writing off the entirety of fictitious monetary claims, such as debt which is rooted in financial derivatives, or other forms of mere gambling debts, now "on the books." The latter obligations must be "torn up and annulled," as in the mode of U.S. financial-bankruptcy proceedings, whenever those claims do not meet the standard of protectionism implicit in the excellent model of the former U.S. Glass-Steagall Act;

c.) defending what is then determined as being valid financial assets, by converting that validated portion of financial claims into values within the bounds and terms of processing of a credit-system of the type consistent with the intent of the Glass-Steagall Act, and as had been specified for the U.S.A. by the proposals for American national banking, by U.S. Treasury Secretary Alexander Hamilton.

Such are the urgent, essential considerations to be applied to promotion of what meets the specifically President Franklin Roosevelt standard for a valid "New Bretton Woods" system. This rule must be applied, specifically to defeating the inherently ruinous, imperialist schemes of monetarist John Maynard Keynes, which had been rudely and summarily rejected by President Franklin Roosevelt, but, despite that, have been inserted by the British asset, U.S. President Harry S Truman.

The implicitly imperialist, present world complex of monetary systems must be replaced now, through a re-organization-in-bankruptcy of the present monetary system, and replaced by a global credit-system consistent, as to matter of physical principle, with the model of U.S. Treasury Secretary Alexander Hamilton's reform. Otherwise, without that action, there is no possibility for a present recovery of the world's principal economies presently existing.

Blame former Federal Reserve Chairman Alan Greenspan for the pain which that reform may prompt; he burned up all the other options.

At the present time, for as long as the presently impossible situation created by the monetarist forms of the present systems of western and central Europe, persists, the actual integration of many parts of the world into the replacement of a monetary system, by a "Hamiltonian" credit-system, must be begun by the initiative of a concert of a limited number of forces composed chiefly of the massive power of persuasion represented by the combination of U.S.A. and certain leading Eurasian nations such as Russia, China, and India.

Even though, otherwise, the nations of western and central Europe, especially those nations which have temporarily abandoned the principle of national sovereignty under demands by London and its accomplices, could not, for that reason, be brought immediately into the general agreements among those other nations whose sovereignty has remained only somewhat intact. Nonetheless, we must acknowledge the right of those nations with such impaired sovereignties, to choose to resume their full former sovereign powers. In such cases of nations which have given up their former sovereignties temporarily, or nations, such as many of those of Africa, which have been long denied true sovereignty by the British empire and that empire's accomplices, we must proceed, nonetheless, if temporarily without them, to the needed international reform, that of a set of credit systems like that prescribed by Hamilton, rather than continue to tolerate obstruction by the relics of inevitably foredoomed, present monetarist systems. This reform, if by only some nations, must be done with our intention of proceeding immediately toward the achievement of the full sovereignty of all nations through the initiative of some nations, as President Franklin Roosevelt had intended that to become the effect of an anti-colonialist, anti-imperialist United Nations Organization (UNO).

In the case of the Americas as a whole, my own, 1982 "Operation Juárez," defines the most appropriate mechanisms for bringing the Americas as a whole into congruence with the defined Eurasian relationship among the keystone states of the U.S.A., Russia, China, India et al.

Those intended relevant actions of global reform, will be sufficient to enable those appropriate reforms made in knowledgeable anticipation of the effects of the immediate reforms by the selected, initiating agency of some nations; all nations, including those nations in Europe whose sovereignty is now crucially impaired by supranational conditionalities, which must be given the implied right of return to their true sovereignty, and their consequent incorporation into the arrangements for the initiating U.S.A.-Eurasia kernel of the more general reform.

The right of all nations to be incorporated, sooner or later, must be protected from the start, as being the rightful opportunities extended, for example, to western and central European states for a status of full parity in their intended ultimate integration into the general reform in progress, as if they had never lost their perfect sovereignties, sovereignties lost as if by some design according to the impulses of such wicked agencies as those jointly, of the British empire's Margaret Thatcher, of U.S. President George H.W. Bush, and of France's President François Mitterand,[35] The relevant principle in this matter, is the principle of proper international law, that, that which is worthy to be believed, is also a form of credit (which includes claims premised on what would have been, morally and under proper law, but which have been the victims of inherently fraudulent

EIRNS

LaRouche's 1982 "Operation Juárez"—a proposal for collaboration among the nations of the Western Hempisphere, including integration of Ibero-America—is a model for the changes needed today. The emphasis is on long-term investment in infrastructure, notably including nuclear power.

elements akin to financial derivatives).

For example, similarly, in the case of Africa, there could be no morally acceptable form of agreement to the new system which did not intend, essentially, to kick the present form of British abuses out of the system, abuses such as Britain's clearly indicated genocidal schemes for that continent. The present British and kindred abusers must be removed entirely from the continent of Africa, bringing benefits for Africa, which were implicitly kindred to those intended for the nations of western and central Europe.[36] In this matter, there is no present British imperial, or kindred special interest which could be allowed to be treated as an exception to the intended universal reform.[37]

What the United Kingdom itself must be given, is the opportunity for practicing honest, scientifically progressive improvement of the conditions of life, health, and productivity of its own citizenry, a devotion better served without what have become the traditionally imperialist, and related practices of that monarchy.

Once Eighteenth-century London had then adopted what were in fact imperial authorities over some nations of the continent of Europe, as it has done, emphatically, under the terms of the February 1763 Peace

---

35. In his last great public address, U.S. President Abraham Lincoln proposed that the former states of the Union must be taken back into the Union with the full rights, as member-states of the Union, which they would have enjoyed had they never left it. The principle of a Pecora Commission is implicitly U.S. constitutional law today, as that notion may be applied to nations whose sovereignty may have been temporarily impaired.

36. The currently vigorous insistence, by a certain circle within the Obama administration, on immediate application of a series of pro-genocidal measures in health care and related policies which that administration has copied, that in exhaustive, expanded, and increasingly exact and elaborated detail, from the Nazi regime of Adolf Hitler, is a crucial error for which the relevant persons and institutions can be neither tolerated nor forgiven. Those elements of the administration must go immediately. Those elements within the administration must be expelled, together with their Nazi-like social and economic policies. The guilty parties are such nations which practiced slavery and the drug trade in opium and kindred habits, associated with the earlier Habsburg, and later Nineteenth-century monarchies of Iberia, the Netherlands, and above all others, the British monarchy, especially that practiced under the British East India Company throughout the existence of that Company and its drug-trafficking successor, the British monarchy still today.

37. You do not approve of this measure? Then it is your misfortune that you have no competence but to accept it, nonetheless.

of Paris, Britain had made itself a virtual empire, initially an empire of the British East India Company, which remains inherently subject, to the present day, to accountability to those nations which it had participated in abusing in that fashion.

The remedy for the case of the Americas as a whole, has been specified by me in my August 1982 "Operation Juárez" draft. That outlined action, presented then, must be slightly adjusted now, to take into account certain more recent developments within the region of that hemisphere as a whole; but, the notion on which that 1982 design was premised, serves as a model of reference for the present moment.

Great emphasis on nuclear power, is an indispensable right for the present development of the future of each and all of the sovereign states of the Americas, in particular, now. This also means an emphasis on long-term investment in building the basic economic infrastructure of economies which are themselves committed to the imperative of advanced technologies based on high energy-flux density-driven development of both infrastructure and comparable technologies.

Without what I have indicated here as the leading role of the U.S.A. in this approach to reform, there would be no hope of escape from a planetary new dark age for any part of humanity as a whole. Were the existing legitimate debt of the U.S. dollar (which should not be permitted to include financial derivatives and related forms of speculation as legitimate) not to be protected in international financial-economic relations, the entire planet would be, in fact, promptly plunged, now, into a hopeless, chain-reaction form of economic disintegration.

These other nations are prisoners-in-fact of the need for the continued viability of outstanding, U.S.-denominated international obligations. Unless the U.S.A. were enabled to satisfy the morally legitimate part of those debts at the same time as promoting its own self-development, even if the benefits to the world at large would be fully realized only over the medium to long term, the U.S.A.'s creditors, in Asia as elsewhere, would be wiped out, and, consequently the world as a whole would be quickly plunged into the kind of a general breakdown-crisis from which existing nations of the planet would cease to exist within their present definitions of nationhood, and the population of the planet would probably shrink from a presently estimated level of 6.7 billions down to the order of two, or even less.

Meanwhile, most of that mass of virtual quadrillions of dubious financial obligations, such as those traced to the cancerous growth of financial-derivatives contracts, must be wiped from the books, by applying the standard of the idea of the U.S. Glass-Steagall Act as a model conception for international application.

Therefore, one should know, with good reason, that if the relevant forces of the British empire do not intend to bring about the termination of what Prince Philip has expressed as the intention of his frankly fascist and imperialist World Wildlife Fund, and his scheme were permitted, the world as a whole is doomed to a prolonged "New Dark Age." His efforts to promote precisely such a "neo-Malthusian" catastrophe, show, that that outcome would be precisely the effect of continuing present British imperial policies, such as those of Prince Philip's Nazi-like World Wildlife Fund, in particular, and, also, the downward trend in health-care policies of the United States and continental Europe, a present trend in Obama Administration policy, which is chiefly an intended expression, on global scale, of not only the Hitler regime, but also that of the Nazi-like, British health-care and related practices, both in Britain, and now intended by London and its dupes within the current Obama administration for the world at large.

One of the several crucial matters to be addressed in this portion of the report, is precisely the implications underlying the specifications which I have just supplied in opening this present chapter of the report as a whole.

The Challenge Now Set Before Us

This report has now come to the matter of the treatment of those notions of physical science which bear heavily on the defining of the remedies for the present world existential quality of economic crisis.

The urgently required, general reform of the world system has two, respectively distinct, but interdependent features.

The first, is the relatively simpler challenge of replacing existing monetary systems entirely, by means of the imposition of a global credit system modeled on the design introduced by Alexander Hamilton. It is urgent that this be extended now, immediately, as promotion of the establishment, or re-establishment of sovereign national credit-systems of the respective nations. This is to be done in a manner bearing on the precedent which the then-future U.S. Treasury Secretary Alexander Hamilton had prescribed in such a form, which was later enacted as the fundamental constitutional principle of a credit, rather than a monetary system, by the Federal Constitution of the U.S. national republic.

The second, more challenging feature, is that of setting the physical-economic parameters for that reformed system which represents the only visible remedy for preventing the presently-in-progress, now-accelerating plunge of the planet toward early arrival at the depths of a general, global economic breakdown-crisis.

On the first account, which I shall address in the following parts of this present chapter, the prescriptions for a credit-system, by Alexander Hamilton, are elementary and clear for anyone who wishes to proceed decently in this matter. I shall refer to those conditions briefly, since the systemically irreconcilable difference between a national credit-system, and an implicitly imperialist monetary system, such as that of Britain's John Maynard Keynes, is, as the case of the adoption of the U.S. Federal Constitution shows, a relatively elementary change in itself, on the condition that the principle of the matter of the included differences is honestly and competently stated.

On the second account, which I treat after that, matters become intellectually more challenging scientifically. There is where, with one qualification, the greater part of the emphasis and discussion of terms of economics as a physical science, instead of a system of financial accounting, must be brought into my report.[38]

First: Credit As Such

On the first account, the crucially significant difficulty challenging most of today's otherwise competent economists, is that the monetarist system is the only system with which most of them have made a familiar habit. Therefore, the efforts of the saner breed of economists and related professionals, prior to the administration of President Richard Nixon, had been focused, chiefly, until March 1, 1968, on the design of the kinds of solutions for problems which had been accepted by the less exotic variety among U.S. economists, as being within the bounds of what was sometimes identified as a "fair trade" model for our U.S.A. financial-economic system as such.[39]

On that account, much the best of what the relevant more competent monetarist economists tend to argue today, had a large degree of approximate competence, for as long as the problems addressed had situated themselves within the bounds of apparently approximate coincidence between what was considered as a working model of the American constitutional credit system of Hamilton et al., and an associated description of the same problem in the terms of a sensible sort of protectionist form of monetary system, both in opposition to the insane and intrinsically immoral free-trade form of the ruinous type asserted by the U.S. Administration of Richard M. Nixon.

Such was the practical issue of our U.S. practice, for as long as the present policy lay within the confines of those restricted pre-conditions. Such was the force of habit, as we encouraged continued respect for that practice even decades after that habit was no longer tolerable.

However, since the inauguration of Nixon, and the wrecking actions of 1971-72 taken by that administration under the guidance of Arthur Burns and George Shultz, such as the terrible, virtually treasonous folly of August 1971, and Shultz's role in the matter of the international monetary system, matters turned radically worse. A "free trade" system emerged, raging through the U.S. and world economy like a destructive force, as under the Trilateral Commission's control of the Carter Administration. One after the other change in policy, such as the unconscionable butchery of the extremely valuable Savings and Loan associations as we see the result of that in the housing crisis of today, had each been more insane than what had been true a short time earlier.

Thus, the Reagan Administration had inherited a regime in which the grip of the Trilateral Commission's poisonous ideology, and, therefore, the approaching deep crisis of the U.S. should have appeared, as virtually inevitable, in the views of astute economists, especially after the first quarter of 1983.

Thus, the pre-1968 conditions of tolerable compromise of a protectionist system with a then-emerging, radically "free market" mode, had ceased to exist. An intrinsically ruinous, radically "free trade" system was substituted under President Nixon. The state of wreckage generated by that and subsequent radical changes,

---

38. As I have noted earlier, whereas physical science is key to our relations to both the Lithosphere and Biosphere, man's relationship to man is located essentially in those principles of Classical poetry and music, which pertain to man's contemplation of man in the Noösphere.

39. The "exotic economists" were typified by followers of the positivists Ernst Mach and the extremist Bertrand Russell, as typified at their worst by the "ivory tower school" of such Russell devotees as Professor Norbert Wiener and John von Neumann.

EIRNS/Stuart Lewis

LaRouche gives his July 25, 2007 webcast. "There is no possibility," he said, "of a non-collapse of the present financial system—none! It's is finished, now! … Only a fundamental and sudden change in the world monetary financial system will prevent a general, immediate chain-reaction type of collapse. At what speed we don't know, but it will go on, and it will be unstoppable!"

has produced what has now become, and that absolutely since the close of July 2007, the present global calamity. Now, every relevant policy adopted by the U.S. government since September 1, 2007, has been, in effect, as what New York City's "Crazy Eddie" praised as "insane."

When the October 1987, 1929-style crash of the Wall Street market hit, that monetary system, which was already very sick, had seemed, nonetheless, to many still, as manageable up to that point. With the October 1987 stock-market crash, the situation became increasingly unmanageable. The economy careened, and that more and more recklessly, under the influence of the incoming of Federal Reserve Chairman Alan Greenspan. With the unleashing of what were implicitly unconstitutional swindles such as "financial derivatives" and the "Y2K" hoax, vast floods of financing poured into markets in the name of averting an alleged bookkeeping-crisis of January 2000; this ruined the banking system, thus marking the approach of the beginning of the end for the very, very sick, present financial system. From that point on, the wildly speculative, implicitly hyper-inflationary "financial derivatives" policies of Paul Volcker's successor as Federal Reserve Chairman, Alan Greenspan, had turned from

what had been a mere swindle, at the outset, into the cancerous unleashing of the utterly, overtly, even flagrantly larcenous, insane wrecking of the very foundations of our own and other banking systems.

So, from since Spring 2000, on, the monetarist form of the present world system as a whole became increasingly unmanageable, despite the distraction against which I had warned publicly on January 3, 2001, which was unleashed by extremely wealthy interests behind "9-11." Since then, the underlying, systemic difference between a monetary system, as such, and a credit system as such, could no longer be reconciled under the same constitutional roof. That change in the state of affairs, has been clearly the case not only for the U.S.A., but globally, since the time of my announcement of such an imminent breakdown of the system, in my international webcast of July 25, 2007.

Now, if those recent trends are continued, one or the other part of the world system as a whole, either the monetary system, or civilization generally, or both, must soon disintegrate. If continuation of the present monetary system in some modified form, were the choice made, as that has been the choice made by the U.S. Obama Administration so far, the U.S. itself, among the similarly perplexed other nations of the world, were virtually already doomed. This fact has been abundantly demonstrated as the relevant current trend, repeatedly, since that time, to the present date.

What the reckless, mentally strange Larry Summers, for example, has failed to grasp, as has Federal Reserve Chairman Bernanke, is that that U.S.A. and British regime of outright stealing, fraud, and other swindle, both public and personal, is now combined with a Hitler-like program of health-care reforms for ridding us of the burden of alleged "useless eaters." All of this has been proceeding on a relative scale far worse than that of Weimar Germany of Summer-Autumn 1923, a calamity which is combined with a health-care program as Nazi as that declared by Adolf Hitler in 1939. This policy of the Obama administration, thus far, is not clearly not the all-American road to recovery; exactly the contrary.

The U.S. Revenue Cutter Massachusetts, *launched in 1791 during Hamilton's term as Treasury Secretary, patrolled the Atlantic coast to protect the precious revenues of the the U.S. Treasury.*

It must be emphasized, therefore, that, however unfortunately, if a monetarist approach were preferred under present conditions, no present economic system of this planet could survive even for the relatively short term immediately ahead. That is the type of condition of what had been known, if only prophetically, in the relevant European literature from the beginning of the Twentieth Century, as "a general breakdown-crisis." This is, presently, the worst crisis of civilization previously experienced in European history since the so-called "New Dark Age" of Europe's Fourteenth Century. Thus, we have now more than reached a roughly comparable point of extreme, global crisis.

Today, only the very silly heads of states and governments would deny that fact, at least not in their private discussions with their most trusted professional confidantes. For Germany, for example, 1923 has returned to run amok again in 2009. Germany is now already *en route* toward an echo of the November of that 1923, this time not only for Germany, but on a global scale. All the nations of western and central Europe, in particular, and beyond, are presently gripped by precisely this, already rampant, accelerating state of affairs.

That much said up to this point, we now proceed toward the meat of the matter, the urgent reform itself.

The American System's Dynamics

Let us now pause in that account, only briefly, before plunging into those deeper scientific issues here which are the core subject-matter of this report, I offer a few very important observations offered to define the setting of the scientific issues as such.

Historically, the essential difference between the American System of political economy, which was developed in a pilot form in the Massachusetts of 1620-1688, as opposed to the traditional European systems prevalent since, remains as a kind of difference between, on the one side, the American tendency, which converges on Alexander Hamilton's vital contribution to the U.S. constitutional system, and, on the opposing side, an intrinsically monetarist, therefore imperialist system, a system which is still reigning in Europe, and, at least, in the last report received on the presently very angered state of mind of President Barack Obama. As I have already pointed out in earlier chapters of this present report, the imperialist character of the prevalent systems of economy of Europe, and also, for this moment, the current U.S. "White House," remains, to this present day, as lodged in the existence and role of all true monetary systems.

The urgently needed general form of remedy for this presently careening global-breakdown crisis, is the elimination of all present vestiges of monetary systems, that just because they are intrinsically imperialist by their axiomatically defined nature as supranational systems. The revival of those presently ruined national economies can occur only through replacement of those monetarist systems by Hamiltonian-like national-credit systems. Otherwise, you, personally, are also soon doomed.

As I have repeatedly emphasized, the new systems must be organized through the establishing of Hamilton types of national banking systems, systems based on a monopoly of the power of the sovereign nation-state to create credit for that sovereign nation, thus banning the continued existence of what are the implicitly imperialist, present international monetary systems.

The required reforms must, therefore, be effected through long-term treaty-agreements, as President Franklin Roosevelt had intended, arrangements which must be associated with a set of fixed exchange-rates of the currencies specific to perfectly sovereign, but cooperating national-banking systems.[40] Notably, President Harry S Truman's implicitly treasonous agreements with Winston Churchill, beginning April 13, 1945, et al., the agreement to subject the U.S.A. itself to the British imperial monetary system of John Maynard Keynes, destroyed the hopes of most of the victims of Anglo-Dutch Liberal imperialist rape, not only in Africa and Asia, but the world more broadly.

Globalization must be thoroughly uprooted. Typical of what must be uprooted, are the relics of a Keynesian imperialist monetarist system which is now hopelessly bankrupt to the degree that there is no present actual hope for any part of humanity without eradicating the form of monetary imperialism presented in the German, 1937 Berlin edition of Keynes' **General Theory**. The now hopelessly bankrupt monetarist systems must be uprooted, and replaced with a Hamiltonian design of a global network of sovereign state-credit-system cooperation among what are, respectively, perfectly sovereign nation-states united by the 1648 Peace of Westphalia, and that Peace's precedent, Nicholas of Cusa's **De Pace Fidei**.

It is, and must become the case for us in the United States, that it is the capital created by the sovereign nation-state, as under the provisions of the U.S. Federal Constitution, which is the only permitted source of the net of uttered domestic currency and debt of the sovereign nation-state. However, this debt can be used, but used properly only under usury-free treaty-agreements of the type inhering in the application of the U.S. Federal Constitution, for long-term credit shared among treaty-partners sharing such a system.

Take the specific cases of Russia and China as illustrations of the principled forms of actions involved.

---

40. It is sufficient that the relative rates of currency valuation must be near to what could be fairly consistent with the relative valuations of a recent period. The crucial issue, for the long term, is not the precise market-valuation, but the nearness to a recent historical set of prices. >From that point of agreement on, it is the rate of development of the economies which had effected that agreement, which is the location of the actually essential interest of the treaty-partners.

Russia & China Now

Russia's and China's are complementary economies. Russia is characterized in a crucial way by the historical development of the nation, since Czar Peter the Great, as through the initiatives, earlier, of Prince Peter the Great's association with the Freiberg which contributed much, as seed-crystals, to the success of Peter's promotion of scientific revolutions. What was recently known, as also during the Soviet times, as the Academies of Science, represent tasks defined by a vast, presently thinly populated territory with vast mineral and other potential, and with the indispensable quality of scientific legacy needed to develop this territory to the combined advantage of its own people and of both its immediate Eurasian neighbors and far beyond. That Russia is the neighbor of a sometimes densely populated set of regions, including the territory of a China which now depends largely on improvements in trading relations with, notably, Russia, Japan, and Korea, and also the U.S.A., combined, for both the mobilization of supply of both mineral resources and science-driver assistance.

The recent commitment of a China which had been lured into use of its relatively cheaper labor force, as one organized to undersell, and replace the output of U.S.A., European, and other locations, resulted in China's vast dependency upon the long-term viability of those, and other, foreign markets for its exports. In the case of China and comparable other cases, "Globalization" has turned out to be not only a terrible mistake, but a grave immediate danger to these nations.

There have been two cruelly ironical outcomes of this experience by China to present date.

There has been, as I have just noted, a collapse in the export markets for China's goods. Under present trends, those foreign markets for China's exports will continue to collapse, and will not only remain collapsed, but continue to fall at accelerating rates, for as long as the present world monetary system is continued, for a generation or more, and also for as long as the present world monetary system exists. In short, China was caught short, as having gained the high-point of its recent export-levels, by selling China exports so cheaply as it had done. Thus, there is no foreseeable long-term recovery for China in any attempted to simply return to those recent export strategies.

There should be no mystery why the London-directed international cartel introduced the policy of "globalization" under which nations living in a semi-colonial past were induced to absorb the function of a cheap-labor market for the elimination of leading industries in North America and Europe. The immediate effect of globalization was the destruction, in Britain's adopted self-interest, of the economies of the nations of North America and Europe, including the former economies of Eastern Europe and the Soviet Union.

The next step was globalization of the world market, such that each nation was forced to rely on purchase and consumption of essential elements of its consumption which had been produced by other nations. Each nation being dependent on a world market controlled by the London-centered cartel of "globalization," was the essence of this swindle, up to a certain point.

Now, another shoe has dropped. At the same time that the margins of monopolist profit by the international swindlers have enriched them, the economies of formerly productive nations, such as those of North America and continental Europe have been looted through this "free trade" system. This has come lately to the point, that the collapse of the nations of the market for China's relevant exports has brought about what is presently a permanent collapse in the economy of China, in particular for as long as current international monetary systems continue to exist.

Back to Growth!

However, under the conditions defined by a turn to the Hamiltonian credit-system, rather than a British-steered imperialist, Keynesian monetarist system, very clear, new qualities of more fortunate opportunities for China's future appear.

Only through the establishment of a Hamiltonian form of international credit-system, could China escape this present trap; and, if China goes so, the world in general, as all of Asia, would dwell in Hell for generations to come.

Admittedly, until a recent time, it has been possible to maintain the form of useful trading relations which pertain to programs of internal development of nations, especially those of so-called developing nations. Many

The success of the new world credit system discussed here requires a primary emphasis on nuclear fission and fusion technologies. Shown here, a test coil being built for the ITER poloidal field coil, at the Naka Fusion Institute in Japan, January 2008.

of the principles expressed in such development are still valid in principle, and are useful references for the future; however, their fault lies in the limitations within which such useful measures are situated. That is to say, that we can use the lessons of this presently limited work on development within and among nations as a kind of "school of technology" which can then be applied, on a larger scale, to a happier global climate for development. The maintaining of an active cadre of qualified specialists in this work today, will be indispensable aid for development on the more serious, broader scale tomorrow. The necessary enlargement of such development programs is no longer possible under the presently collapsing, world, pro-Keynesian system.

Once we have said and understood that qualifying observation, we are free to consider the larger reality of today.

The issue so posed, is: how much development, both in quality and in scale, represents a well-defined technological development program, as much as of a break-even level of development of a nation? China needs expansion in productive powers of labor, per capita and per square kilometer even more than it clearly does require growth in the scale of useful production and services. This can not be done without a physical, capital-intensive transformation.

China requires long-term physical capitalization of a shift into in-depth, capital-intensive modes of development of its population as whole. We are speaking of a period of capital development of the productive forces of China, per capita, and per square kilometer, during an initial, interim period of about a half a century. This means two generations of step-wise increase of the culturally determined productive powers of the population, combined with a relevant inflow of raw materials, and also an increasingly capital-intensive accumulation of investment in physical capital relevant to production.

The design of such an urgently needed reform in perspective is not possible under any system with the intrinsically imperialist characteristics of a Keynesian or comparable international monetary system. No competent remedies would be possible under a continuation of that presently London-dominated world imperial system, especially for as long as President Obama remains a victim of that British imperialist monetarist system.

Under the introduction of a Hamiltonian credit-system, and excluding a Keynesian or kindred monetary system, as President Franklin Roosevelt had intended, China's neighbors Russia, and other former associates of the Soviet Union, Korea, and Japan, and the U.S.A. and Europe, must be regarded as the principal sources of capitalized credit and technological cooperation uttered for global development. The goal of such development must be in the order of a century of fair estimates and a more definite half-century of intentions supported by treaty-agreements under a world credit-system, now replacing the presently dying monetary system. The possibility of success of such a program demands a primary emphasis on nuclear-fission and thermonuclear-fusion sources of power, as being the specific modalities corresponding to the degree of a physical-chemistry of development and defined potential energy-flux density required to support the technologies which are indispensable for such a program of a half-century to century-long perspectives. This also requires the immediate reserving of plutonium-supplies for charging uranium and thorium nuclear reactors in Asia as in other parts of our gravely troubled world.[41]

To realize those objectives for China and Russia, there must be a vigorous rebuilding of the cultural potential for high-technology development within western and central Europe and North America. This case for Russia and China is paradigmatic for the urgent reform of the world credit-system as a whole

Explication in related directions, for other exemplary cases, is sufficiently well implied. Therefore, return for consideration of the example I just indicated, to attention to the matter of the global implications of the system of long-term, fixed-exchange-rate-driven capital formation, which the case for China, just summarized, implies.

Under the urgently needed, happy reform,. we will be, admittedly, building a vast capital debt as a result of the uttering of debt-based, very high-technology capital formation within the uttering by national-banking systems. However, under the replacement of the present global, and now hopelessly bankrupt monetary system, by a fraternal system of Hamiltonian credit-systems, this debt will be secured by the created actually physical, productive and closely related assets it has been used to create, and by the debtors' gain of the means, through gains in per-capita productivity, to sustain that growing debt with greater comfort and security in each nation's own sovereign powers.

Instead of building a debt to alien, imperialist interests, the debt will be based on credit shared among sovereign nations in the mutual economic and related interests of those nations themselves. Such was always the specific intention of the American System as informed by the reforms introduced by Alexander Hamilton.

We must think in terms of physical economy, primarily, and enslave money-economy to the service of those physical-economic goals.

The U.S.A.: History & Perspective

This will be a realization of the benefit of the inherent superiority of the traditional, Hamiltonian, American constitutional method, a method, which has suc-

---

41. Since any future warfare among leading powers would be a thermonuclear war from which little would survive, it is not necessary to reserve plutonium stocks for preparing for a war which everyone would lose. Such wars must be prevented. It is important to note here, that the imperialist method has depended, since the Peloponnesian War, on inducing intended victims to destroy one another, so that the real imperial force, such as the Anglo-Dutch Liberal financier gang, might gain and hold onto ruling imperial power. Next time, instead of a new "Seven Years War," invade Britain immediately, instead. The mere decision to adopt such a strategic policy, would keep the Anglo-Dutch agencies from pursing the traditional method associated with the name of Julian the Apostate.

ceeded whenever adopted and employed by the U.S.A., as in that revival of the U.S.A. economy under President Franklin Roosevelt which came after the ruin of that economy earlier, as under the Anglophile policies of such defective Presidents as (actually) Theodore Roosevelt, Wilson, Coolidge, and Hoover.

This idea of a credit-system, rather than a European monetary system, had soon built up, from its inception, a fragile colony along the Atlantic coast of North America, to develop into becoming the once-mighty nation which had become the greatest economic power the world might have imagined up to the time of Franklin Roosevelt's death.

The admittedly onerous price that must be paid for recovery of both the presently bankrupted world economic and monetary systems, is the urgently immediate termination of that hoax of Britain's Prince Philip called "environmentalism." For, if we do not uproot and terminate that intrinsically fraudulent ideology, it were inevitable that the world as a whole would, indeed, degenerate immediately into a global "new dark age," under which clearly fascistic Prince Philip's stated goal, of reducing the world population from a presently estimated 6.7 billions persons, to less than two billions, would be realized, beginning with a rather immediate effect felt like a sudden jerk, over a mere two or slightly more generations. This would cause a far-greater genocide than was launched, by exactly the same policies as, for the present moment, at least, the present Obama administration, the exact same domestic social policies which Adolf Hitler, writing in his own hand, introduced to Germany in 1939. Hence, the pre-planned mass-murder health-care policies which the Obama administration has presently imported from the United Kingdom.

Obviously, the present Obama administration will not survive much longer, unless it soon changes its policies, away from the Hitler-copied policies of the circles of Larry Summers and the behaviorist psychologists such as Peter Orszag and Rahm and Ezekiel Emanuel, into the new directions which I have outlined

The head of British East India Company operations, Prime Minister Lord Shelburne (1737-1805), adopted the "divide and rule" methods of the Roman Emperor Julian the Apostate. Tony Blair follows the same tradition today.

here. The full effect of the currently onrushing general, world breakdown-crisis is already approaching at a highly accelerated rate.

Mass-murderous health-care policies, such as those which had been intended, for 2005, by the George W. Bush, Jr., administration, are once again on the launching-pad, this time by the Obama administration. The rates of mass-murder of U.S. citizens, by Hitler methods, are already pre-planned in the fairly calculable effects of the inherently mass-murderous copies of specific Adolf Hitler policies already uttered by the Obama administration, especially by the freak-show of the gang associated with the prospective "Adolf Eichmann-like" expression of that administration's curiously perverse bent, toupéed Peter Orszag. These policies are not, of course, original to either Hitler's Germany or Obama's U.S.A.; they were then, as today, primarily British, policies which had been copied, in conception, by a Hitler regime which had been created, in fact, by the British monarchy, as that pattern is now being echoed in other parts of Europe already, today.[42]

The Deeper, Physical Policies

There is no rational form of "natural" money-price in economies. As economic history since August 1971 has demonstrated, a "free trade" system is, by nature, the most immoral, most crooked of all gambling systems, run, almost inevitably, and almost invariably, by the most crooked and most powerful manipulators in the international system.

Most societies known to historians today, as in the cases of ancient Asian empires and such expressions as the Delphi Apollo cult, expressed cultures of what came to be named as representing the "oligarchical model"

---

42. After all, it was the British empire which actually created Benito Mussolini and Adolf Hitler, just as London was the center of radiation of similar-to-Hitlerian population-management policies of the same Harriman family which played a leading role, together with the Bank of England's Montagu Norman, in crafting the placing of Adolf Hitler into power in Germany.

associated with the Delphi cult's role in orchestration of the war between the two would-be maritime imperialist powers, over monetary primacy, of Athens versus Sparta. Such was the intent expressed by British adoption of the named tradition of Julian the Apostate by the Lord Shelburne who is the putative predecessor of Britain's morally degenerate Tony Blair.

The wars which engaged a foolish French King Louis XIV, and, then, the Seven Years War, the Napoleonic wars, and such later wars launched by the British empire, as the Japan wars against, successively, China, Korea, and Russia, beginning 1895, the British use of the silly Habsburg Kaiser to spark the Balkan wars, World War I, World War II, the so-called "Cold War," the perpetual state of warfare in Southwest Asia since 1945-46, and the Iraq wars, are each and all examples of religious, or quasi-religious wars, which the British Empire has orchestrated according to its adoption of the tradition of the Roman Emperor Julian the Apostate. Such were those Napoleonic wars, orchestrated by Britain's European freemasonic channels, from which Britain emerged, at the expense of foes and allies alike, as the dominant imperial force in the world, a wave of wars which continued until the time of London's defeat by a United States led by President Abraham Lincoln, over the British empire. Thus, the British responded to President Lincoln's victory geopolitically, by creating a series of what became, since the ouster of Bismarck, in 1890, every major war fought on this planet, since then, to the present day, especially long and worse than useless, wasting wars in the likeness of H.G. Wells' "The Shape of Things to Come." Such was the meaning of Britain's 1890 ouster of Germany's Chancellor Otto Bismarck, which started all the major and local wasting warfare since that time, including the threats implicit in an attempted fascist takeover of the administration of President Barack Obama, by the British empire with its Hitlerian policies of genocide through health-care and pension "reform" of today.

Credit & Physical Systems

My emphasis on a credit-system, is not intended to suggest that the price of money has no meaning. The use of money, and the use of the price assigned to it, have effects; but the mere value attributed to money is a color of a different horse. *As I shall emphasize in this present chapter of the report, true economic value is, functionally, physical, not monetary.*

This brings us to focus our attention on the second great categorical implications of a Hamiltonian appreciation of the role of a credit system and the true meaning of "economic value." To reach that goal, we must define the relevant relations in physical terms, and, after that, show the way in which physical considerations lead toward the effects shown as the functionally determined relations among prices.

For this purpose, we living today have the great historical advantage given to us, for this purpose, by what I have referenced earlier here as what I have already emphasized as the role of Academician V.I. Vernadsky's conception of the physical-scientific relations among Lithosphere, Biosphere, and Noösphere.[43]

The Noösphere As an Economy

As I have emphasized in reports featured in earlier chapters of this present report, if we are speaking in competent, ontological terms of reference, no economy is a money-economy, but a physical economy. Those qualities of change which distinguish the human, from an animal species. can not be competently identified, until, and unless we focus on the significance of the uniquely human power of creativity which distinguishes the human individual from members of all other species.

Today, there is no competent form of modern notion of economy, outside the context of what emerged as Academician V.I. Vernadsky's uniquely original ontological definitions of the distinction of the ontologically abiotic segment of the Biosphere from the ontologically abiotic segment of the Lithosphere, and of the ontological distinction of the human species' Noösphere from all other forms of life.

The first step to be taken, in reflections on that body of evidence, is to recognize the role of what is uniquely specific to human individual creativity, in its relationship to, and specific quality of impact on the Biosphere. This set of distinctions provides the framework, within physical science, for today's only competent notion of the meaning of *economy*. All related categorical topics of economy must be confined within the role of the uniquely creative powers of the human individual in creating the phenomena which distinguish the changes occurring as the effect of the Noösphere, from the potential relative population-density within the Biosphere. Here, not in money *per se*, nor within the realm of statistical processes associated with money, lies the

---

43. I have addressed this matter in locations published earlier.

Hieronymus Bosch's triptych, "Garden of Earthly Delights" (c. 1500) captures the quality of depravity that also came to dominate our culture after World War II. "The depravity is expressed most nakedly," LaRouche writes, "in the moral cancer of belief in an intrinsic value of money."

essence of any competent discussion of the determining characteristics of political-economy in today's world.

In fact, this has always been true; the difference between then and now, is that, as a matter of science, or making the policy of our U.S.A., there is no longer any forgiveable reason for not knowing that this is true.

What I have just said here, can begin to be appreciated more adequately, by presenting a selected few of the points of argument which I have referenced either earlier in this present report, or in earlier publications. As follows.

First, the biosphere: even in past times before the existence of the human species has been known by the evidence of paleontology, the development of the Biosphere's array of participating species, was increasing the ration of the Biosphere as a whole relative to the Lithosphere as a whole. In the examining of evidence from ancient times, the paleontologist's best proof of the distinction of archeological man from apes, was a fire-side; only the mind of man uses "fire" in any of those expressions reaching toward thermonuclear fusion, and, perhaps, matter-anti-matter reactions. The difference between man and ape, is that human beings are essentially Prometheans.

One of the most important steps taken for the purpose of defining that distinction more rigorously, is made by reference to relevant evidence bearing on the composition of the so-called periodic table of physical chemistry, or, better said, physical biochemistry. What portion of the mass of the planet is represented by material which is either living, or clearly remains of living creatures, or represents items in the periodic table which are specific to the physical chemistry of isotopes or kindred phenomena which are specific to living processes?

Second, when we juxtapose the growth of the Biosphere to the Noösphere, what is the ratio of the Noösphere to the Biosphere in which it has appeared? What are the rates of change in these ratios as considered relative to the current relative mass of each and of both combined?

To be as brief as possible, the Biosphere reflects a principle of life, which tends to result in an increase of the Biosphere, relative to the Lithosphere, whereas the increase of the productive powers of labor requires, and produces an increase of the ratio of the Noösphere to the Biosphere. Such evidence defines the meaning of what may be termed, alternately, as the anti-entropy of life, or, in the higher phase-space domain, of human creativity.

So, the existence of the manifestation of human scientific-technological progress, is to be found in the increase of the Biosphere relative to the Lithosphere, and as the progressive development of the Noösphere increases the cumulative development of the Biosphere. The difference between the Biosphere and Noösphere, in this respect, is that the increase of the Biosphere in itself, is physical, or, as we say, "involuntary;" but, that the rate of increase of Biosphere otherwise, is effected through the action represented by the voluntary human activity driving the growth of the Noösphere which occurs solely through the factor of willful human activity.

These considerations point our attention, upwards, to some crucially significant higher considerations.

However, although all that I have presented, above, just now, tends to induce complacency respecting our required attention to some even much more significant kinds of evidence. These are matters which bear on the crucial role of Classical forms of artistic composition in physical science, such as the Classical music represented by the discoveries of J.S. Bach, and the great Classical poetry, such as that, for English or German speakers, of Shakespeare, Shelley, and Friedrich Schiller.

When science looks down toward the subject-matter which we, conventionally, consider respectively non-living and living processes, we employ the methods of physical science. However, when we are focussed upon the subject of the social expression of the mental processes wherein the power of physical-scientific discovery resides, sanity lies only in the domain of those forms of Classical artistic composition associated with music and poetry, or the work of great Classical painters such as Leonardo da Vinci, Rafael Sanzio, and the genius of Rembrandt.

In those latter aspects of the expression of the role of Classical modes of artistic composition, it is the human mind as such, which becomes for us the essence of the subject of physical science of the properly conceived universe as a whole. Hence the self-destruction of European culture in Europe and the Americas, since the inauguration of President Harry S Truman, must be attributed to those intrinsically malicious forms of systemic insanity typified, in the post-Franklin Roosevelt world, by the moral depravity intrinsic to the rising post-war influence of existentialism in general and its depraved expression in forms typified by the post-war Congress for Cultural Freedom. It is the sick, sick way, in which man has come to degrade man as man, which has been the root of the evils of our time, as it was in such manifestations as the rise of fascism in Italy and Germany under the prevalent depravity of post-World War I conditions.

The more general expression of such forms of depravity lies in the pathetic attention to the delusion of money which has been the essential characteristic of all imperial systems of rule up to the present time. The depravity is expressed most nakedly in the moral cancer of belief in an intrinsic value of money.

Economy & Creativity

Take the case of Johannes Kepler's uniquely original principle of gravitation, in his **The Harmonies of the World**. Review that discovery by Kepler from the vantage-point presented for the principle of the tensor applied to experimental evidence, by Albert Einstein. For this purpose, look at the tensor from the standpoint of its ontological expression as a physical principle, rather than merely a mathematical form of procedure. The importance of doing this, as for the purposes of the domain of physical economy, is to grasp the essential aspect of Kepler's genius in making his uniquely original discovery of the physical principle of gravitation.

Unfortunately, under the influence of the empiricist methods derived from initiatives of Paolo Sarpi, the modern classroom tends to locate the discovery of what is truly the footprint of a universal physical, or related principle, in the mathematical formulations themselves. The student so misguided tends not to hear what Einstein was actually saying. The formula does not generate the principle of gravitation; rather, the mathematical expression for the manifestation of gravitation is an adumbrated shadow of the principled action which has generated the perceptible, or quasi-perceptible description of the sensed effect of gravitation.

Admittedly, the Eighteenth-century and early-to-middle Nineteenth-century mathematicians seem solidly sane, if only when compared with positivists such as Ernst Mach or such, ontologically, utterly deranged devotees of Bertrand Russell as Professor Norbert Wiener and John von Neumann, Typically, the usual modern mathematician and his like are so thoroughly brain-washed on this account, such that they fail to recognize that our sense-perceptions, are like the laboratory instruments by which we supplement those senses, are merely instruments which measure effects, rather than representing directly that principle of action which causes the effects.

Since the subject of economy is human behavior, rather than that of mere mathematicians who have transformed themselves into self-made mere abstractions, as mere shadows of reality, rather than actually human in their academic and related behavior, the long reign of empiricism, since the rise of Sarpi in late Sixteenth-century Europe, called the "Liberalism" of such wicked quacks as Adam Smith and Jeremy Bentham, has had its virtually decorticating effect on much of what passed for well-educated learning today. So, the idea of money found in the mouth of the all-too-typical modern mathematical economist, is the typical source of the intellectual incompetence of the relevant typical specialist and relevant official of today.

Economy is essentially physical economy, and the action which defines economy as a process, is essentially human creativity as typified by such fellows as Nicholas of Cusa, Leonardo da Vinci, Johannes Kepler, Pierre de Fermat, Gottfried Leibniz, Abraham Kästner, Carl F. Gauss, Bernhard Riemann, Max Planck, Albert Einstein, and Academician V.I. Vernadsky. It is the discovery of both the fact and the employment of those new physical principles which could never be discovered by deductive methods of thinking, which is the only competent basis for defining either the principles of economy, or effecting the ability of mankind to gain net progress in the productive powers of mankind over attrition.

The principle of creativity, which is also relative to economy as such, does not lie within the bounds of a reductionist form of mathematical argument. On this account, it used to be recognized, especially since the powerful impact of the discoveries of Johann Sebastian Bach on his students and successors of the Eighteenth and Nineteenth centuries, that, since that impassioned commitment to both Classical poetry and musical composition in the principles of well-tempered musical composition in the Florentine Renaissance tradition of tuning, and also in the related role of Classical poetry, these were once the primary site of human individual creativity among the leading strata of the general population. Albert Einstein performing the violin rather regularly in the great Berlin synagogue concurs with such evidence.

It has been through the loss of effective connection in the education of the young, in the decadence which grew up during the Twentieth Century, and grew so ferociously under the influence of the existentialism of Theodor Adorno et al. and Europe's Congress for Freedom, that there was a grave loss of access to those powers of the mind associated with Classical artistic composition and its performance. It had been, since as long ago as we are familiar with European cultures in particular, that the Classical artistic tradition, as typified by Classical modalities in poetry and song, is the principal area of the human cognitive function from which true creativity spills over into physical science and competent notions and practices of economic progress.

Why Human Life Is Sacred

The most thoroughly evil among all of the many blunders of policy exhibited by the administration of President Obama thus far, has been his rage-driven passion for killing what his advisors, such as a virtually reborn flunky for Himmler, Peter Orszag treat as "useless eaters." In fact, in all essential features, the stated Obama policy on health-care and pensions is identical, in every implication of practice, with the infamous policy which Chancellor Adolf Hitler both composed and uttered ,on the subject of "lives not worthy to be lived," immediately upon his declaration of what became known as "World War II." There is absolutely no margin of error in that statement by me.

Obama is reported to be increasingly very angered against me because of my truthful and relevant statements on his policy utterances since his infamous journey, not quite like Dick Whittington's cat, to visit the Queen, a Queen married to the most monstrous advocate of mass genocide living on this planet today, the World Wildlife Fund's Prince Philip, a Prince Philip whose Hitler-like policies are faithful replicas of the similar bestiality of the policies of Bertrand Russell.

I must consider anyone who attacks me for what I have said on that issue as lacking any proverbial "leg to stand on" in this matter at issue.

My strong suggestion is that Obama's rage against me is not because he desires to perpetrate a policy of genocide identical with that launched by Adolf Hitler, but because I had attacked his personal ego, *his* policy. If that is the case, and the available evidence points, predominantly in that direction, his crime were worse, worse because the criminality he introduces is not motivated by a wish to perpetrate genocide, but, if he is not pro-genocidal, were like that of the Emperor Nero, to cause great death for no other reason than satisfy his ego. In that, I would hope I am mistaken, for the sake of us all.